ORLANDO
THEN & NOW

ORLANDO THEN & NOW

STEPHEN EVANS

THUNDER BAY
P·R·E·S·S

San Diego, California

Thunder Bay Press
An imprint of the Advantage Publishers Group
5880 Oberlin Drive, San Diego, CA 92121-4794
www.thunderbaybooks.com

Produced by Salamander Books,
an imprint of Anova Books Ltd
151 Freston Road
London W10 6TH, United Kingdom

"Then and Now" is a registered trademark of Anova Books Ltd.

© 2007 Salamander Books

All notations of errors or omissions should be addressed to Thunder Bay Press,
Editorial Department, at the above address. All other correspondence (author
inquiries, permissions) concerning the content of this book should be addressed
to PRC Publishing, 151 Freston Road, London W10 6TH, United Kingdom.

ISBN-13: 978-1-59223-785-2
ISBN-10: 1-59223-785-1

Library of Congress Cataloging-in-Publication Data available upon request.

1 2 3 4 5 11 10 09 08 07

Printed in China.

ACKNOWLEDGMENTS

While many helped, I would like to formally thank the following persons for assisting me with this project.
Foremost, and primarily, I need to thank Stephanie Gaub, photo archivist at the Orange County Regional
History Center, for providing dozens of options to me in a very limited amount of time. Stephanie not only
pulled images from the files with little or no warning but did so more pleasantly than I dared hope anyone
would. Another pleasant surprise was photographer Simon Clay, who tried his best to run me ragged for two
days while taking nearly all of the present-day photos. Simon went so far as to find and rent a small boat,
take us out into Lake Monroe, and climb atop an abandoned wharf for one photo—that's ingenuity *and*
dedication. Speaking of effort, I need to thank my buddy Larry. Before Simon and I traveled the
countryside, Larry accompanied me on a preliminary research trek across the three-county area that makes
up Orlando. Our mission was not easy: to locate the sites of our historic photos and then to debate what
positions—without any surviving references, in many cases—had been used to take them. Fortunately, most
of our efforts were not in vain. Thank you for the company and the assistance. In the realm of research, I
would like to thank Tana Porter at the OCRHC and the staff of the Winter Park Public Library, but I owe a
special nod to Kim Peters for reminding me that some librarians *do* still have the courtesy, patience, and
professionalism that librarians used to have. Kim seems to reside in the local history stacks on the fourth
floor of the Orlando public library. She continued looking for information even after I ran out of ideas,
hope, and time. I also want to recognize the largely volunteer efforts that have been made by the Central
Florida Heritage Foundation in creating *Orlando: A Visual History* and by Steve Rajtar in researching,
compiling, and posting his series of trail guides; both of these resources are available on the Internet.
Finally, I would like to thank Allison, the faithful client I had to reschedule and reschedule to stay focused
on this project. Allison finally went so far as to start planning her wedding instead of continuing work on
her novel while waiting on me! And, lastly, thank you, partner, for supporting us during the few months it
took to work on this project. (NB: captions for pages 136 to 143 supplied by Salamander editorial.)

PICTURE CREDITS

The publisher wishes to thank the following for kindly supplying the photographs that appear in this book:

Then photographs:
All Then photographs are courtesy of the Historical Society of Central Florida, except for the following:
Library of Congress, Prints and Photographs Division: p. 22 [LC-D4-33526], p. 24 [LC-D418-9409], p. 26
[LC-D4-33527], p. 120 [HABS FLA,48-WIPA,1-6], p. 124 [LC-USZ62-57600], p. 126 [LC-USZ6-1707].
Florida State Archives: p. 136, p. 138, p. 140. Bettmann/Corbis: p. 142.

Now photographs:
All Now images were taken by Simon Clay (© Anova Image Library), except for the following:
Joseph R. Melanson, Aerials Only Gallery: p. 137. Blaine Harrington III/Corbis: p. 139. Forestier
Yves/Corbis Sygma: p. 141. Corbis: p. 143.

INTRODUCTION

Like the roots of many towns that grew up in what was then known as Mosquito County and thought of as southern Florida, the roots of Orlando sprang from a fort that was part of a proposed and ever-evolving but never finished network of American fortifications. These forts were intended to provide protection to nearby settlers and were planned to be a day's journey apart from each other so that all settlers would be within easy reach of one. The more prominent forts in the local area were Fort Christmas (to the east), Fort Maitland (to the immediate north), Fort Monroe (later Fort Mellon, near present-day Sanford, to the more distant north), and Fort Gatlin.

Fort Gatlin was a stockaded fort built on a small rise of land between Lake Gatlin, Lake Jennie Jewel, and Lake Gem Mary. Fort Gatlin's namesake was an assistant army surgeon by the name of Henry Gatlin, who was one of 105 soldiers killed in an ambush carried out by Seminole warriors on December 28, 1835. The name Orlando, according to one local legend, was also rooted in a Seminole War death: a young sentinel named Orlando Reeves, who allegedly sacrificed his life by yelling to wake his comrades and announce an ambush near what has become Lake Eola in downtown Orlando.

Seven years after the end of the "second" Seminole War (1835–1842), in November 1849, Fort Gatlin was closed. Since the soldiers were confident that troubles with the Seminoles were behind them, many decided to stay on and to relocate their families to the area. The settlement that grew up close to the fort became known as Jernigan, named after Aaron and Isaac Jernigan, two pioneer cattlemen who had arrived in 1843 with 700 head of cattle.

Two events took place in 1857 that were instrumental in determining the future of Jernigan. First, in September, a post office was authorized about three and a half miles north of the settlement, at the intersection of a supply road that ran from Fort Mellon to Fort Brooke (near present-day Tampa) and the better-known Gadsden's Trail that ran from Fort Butler (present-day Astor) to Fort Lloyd (near the northeast shore of Lake Okeechobee) and points north and south. Second, in October, a landholder named Benjamin F. Caldwell deeded four acres of land he held in that vicinity to be used by the county. The new settlement that sprang up there became known as Orlando.

Natural disasters, like major hurricanes in August 1893, September 1894, and August 1899, took their toll on the growing community. Most notable were the twin freezes in late December 1894 and on February 7, 1895, when the temperature plummeted from a daytime high of 85°F to an overnight morning low of 17°F. The freezes killed virtually every citrus tree in the county and bankrupted seven of eight local banks. Growers, pickers, packagers, and shippers, as well as their suppliers and supporters, were suddenly out of business. A large number of them, and their families, left town, penniless and discouraged. But that disaster had one far-reaching result: it forced the young city to diversify its economy. Probably more than any other event, the Big Freeze, as the freezes of that winter came to be called, caused Orlando to develop into a regional city.

Sure, the city replanted its citrus trees—that was a business the people knew. But while those newly planted groves matured, residents returned to cattle raising, expanded their lumber and turpentine interests, and experimented with a variety of other farm crops. Perhaps most importantly, the city's board of trade increased its efforts to promote the city as a healthy retreat, a tourist destination, and a winter home to northerners. As part of one of those efforts, a contest was held to update the city's nickname. In 1908, Orlando became the "City Beautiful," a name that continues to be used almost a century later.

On the road to recovery, Orlando's population and economy grew. The number of permanent residents tripled between 1910 and 1920 and again between 1920 and 1930. During those years, the city experienced a remarkable land boom that changed its image and its focus. Several large residential areas stretched the city on the ground, while the business district grew taller, more impressive, and more important.

Also impressive were new networks of state roads and national highways that led to and passed through Orlando. The Dixie Highway network was first. It provided two signed routes—one from Michigan, another from Chicago—that brought waves of "tin can tourists" into the area. These early auto tourists carried their own food with them, much of it in tin cans, and camped in fields alongside the roadways. Before long, roadside motels and restaurants with automobile parking lots, as well as campgrounds and rest stops, sprang up to accommodate this new type of traveler.

With additional highway improvements and the acceptance of air travel by the general public, Orlando's spot as a tourist destination was sealed. Cypress Gardens, Gatorland, Xanadu, the Prince of Peace Memorial, Weeki Wachee, Silver Springs, Six Gun Territory, Circus World, and Masterpiece Gardens were some of the original attractions that drew early tourists to the area. Then, in the late 1960s, Walt Disney World came to town, and the Orlando area was never to be the same again.

When Orlando incorporated in 1875, the town was still barely habitable—even by standards of the times. It had much more in common with the legendary wild west of cowboys and Indians and grassy ranges and cattle ranches than it did with the rest of America. In addition to wildness, the exploration and settlement of this part of the state (which was then known as South Florida because the expanse of the Everglades began not far beyond Kissimmee) were complicated by its subtropical heat and humidity, its swarms of mosquitoes and other insects, and its terrain of swamplands and "palmetto prairies." This photograph of the primary north-south thoroughfare, Orange Avenue, is thought to date from 1879, when the city's population was approximately 200. It is the earliest known image of the new settlement. The home in the distance, beyond the trails that became Central Avenue (to the left) and Wall Street (to the right), was the home of former Confederate Captain Thomas J. Shine.

Four blocks north of Church Street, then the main westward artery in town, Thomas Shine's home was considered to be in the "country." Now, after more than a century as Orlando's main street and its physical, ceremonial, and cultural center, Orange Avenue is no longer a twisted, sandy, rutted trail that wanders a short distance from orange groves on the north side of town to a lake on the south. This present-day view, from the same general place and in a similar direction (though from a higher vantage point), demonstrates that the original road continues to be an important anchor—for a region that served more than 1,600,000 people in the year 2000.

The old town well on the southwest corner of the courthouse square was built by Jacob "Jake" Summerlin to provide water for the residents (animals included) of Orlando. The well, which was lined with top-quality terra-cotta, was forty-two feet deep and topped with an elaborate well house that had a wood-shingle roof. It was dug sometime after the 1875 courthouse was built, probably between 1880 and 1883. Water from the well was drawn with two buckets that were raised and lowered on a pulley and chain system. The well was always a gathering place for buyers and sellers and talkers and debaters. In fact, a soapbox and public stumping stage was erected in this area for a time. The armory and public market were nearby, as well as Jacob R. Cohen's general store and a few private residences. The center of town was still a block or two south, along Pine Street and West Church Street.

The first water system (the Orlando Water Company) was started in 1886, and the old town well was filled in. Water mains and fire hydrants were placed in 1886, and a tall, cylindrical holding tank, or tower, known as "the standpipe" was erected on the southwest corner of Orange Avenue and Marks Street the next year. Water was pumped into the open standpipe and stored there until it was drained into the network of water mains through use. The weight of the water in the tank provided the system's pressure. For many years, local legend says, the standpipe could not be completely filled because the pump was not strong enough to overpower a certain amount of pressure. During fires, water was pumped into the standpipe continuously to maintain a constant pressure. (In addition, a separate cistern at Orange Avenue and Pine Street provided a backup source of water.) The area where the old town well—and the 1875 and 1892 courthouses—stood is now a park. This bus shelter stands on one edge of that park. The back side of the Premiere Trade Center Towers looms in the background, along with the top few floors of the bank building at SunTrust Center.

At the time of this photo (ca. 1884–1886), Pine Street was the primary eastward route into and out of Orlando. Heading east from this intersection at Orange Avenue, travelers could reach the Fort Gatlin–Jernigan area and the sizable Conway area population, as well as Narcoosee, St. Cloud, and the east coast. The Charleston House (on the right; known earlier as the Lucky House) was the most prominent landmark at this intersection until the Watkins Block replaced it in 1895. Like the other streets downtown, Pine Street was made of sand, but because it was such a major street, it was widened by ten feet in 1883 and paved with clay in 1891. Bricks were put down from Main Street to West Street in 1908. Many of the original wooden buildings on the eastern end of Pine Street were destroyed or damaged by the 1884 fire. Following that fire, the city adopted its first building codes, which required building exteriors to be made of masonry or brick.

Today, Pine Street is just another downtown street. The Charleston House is gone, as is the Watkins Block that replaced it. That building, by James L. Giles, was the largest brick office structure in town when it was completed. The north face of the new Premiere Trade Center Towers has even taken the site of Milo Cooper's barbershop, which, throughout the 1880s, stood on the lot behind the Charleston House. Cooper was a former slave who served only white customers. The next establishment was a large livery stable. A. M. Hyer bought this livery in 1870, then sold it to James J. Patrick in 1878. Across the street in 1878 stood Dr. Foster Chapman's pharmacy. Chapman's drugstore had no front—he said the weather never got cold enough and he never needed to close, so why bother? It is said that half of the city's political issues were debated here. The other half were discussed at Foster's Livery Stable at the southwest corner of Orange and Central. The historical structures that remain in the area are now, as they have traditionally been, offices and restaurants for lawyers and government workers.

Cassius A. Boone, a direct descendant of American trailblazer Daniel Boone, came to Orlando in 1870 at the age of twenty. He moved in with his aunt (Mary Boone Bryson, who lived on East Central Avenue) and became one of the first teachers in the school at the Union Free Church. Before long, he partnered with William A. Patrick to start a hardware store on the northeast corner of Church Street and Orange Avenue, then the center of town. Officially, the store was C. A. Boone and Company, but on the street it was known as Boone Hardware almost as long as the building (shown here in 1887) stood—even after Joseph L. Guernsey took over the business in the mid-1890s (local legend says that Boone traded it for an orange grove that Guernsey owned). Guernsey and his four sons ran the business, already one of the largest hardware stores in the state, until his death in 1922. At that time, the sons sold out to their longtime (since the late 1880s) rival, Bumby Hardware.

The old Boone Hardware building, which had finally become known as the Guernsey Block, was demolished in July 1924 to make way for a new F. W. Woolworth's store. That two-story building was completely finished in terra-cotta. As in most cities across the country, the Woolworth's lunch counter in Orlando was a centerpiece in the fight for equal civil rights. The largest such demonstration took place on March 6, 1960, when six black youths approached the counter and took seats. The counter was closed down until the youths left. Unlike demonstrations in other Florida cities, no police were summoned and no violence broke out. The Woolworth's building was demolished in January 2004. When completed, the new Premiere Trade Center Towers building will occupy the entire block on the east side of Orange Avenue from Pine Street to Church.

Church Street (shown here looking west from Orange Avenue in 1887) was originally the main route between homesteads and towns to the west and the center of town. Church Street led in the direction of Ocoee, Winter Garden, Oakland, Gotha, and Clermont. It was also the commercial and financial center of the new town, and, when the railroad came in 1880, the transportation center as well. As the center of commerce, the street was home to nearly any kind of business a town might need. Church Street was the financial center because the first "bank" in Orlando was located here—W. G. White's general store (the first building on the left). White had secured a large iron safe for use in his store. With nowhere else to turn, his customers asked him to keep money and valuables for them. Finally, as home to the first three train stations and the southern terminus of the short-lived trolley system, this was the transportation hub.

As the commercial center of Orlando, Church Street provided addresses for retail establishments—clothing stores, a livery stable, a harness maker, a furniture store, restaurants, groceries, fruit and vegetable vendors, confectioners, a baker, a Chinese laundry, a barber, a tailor, a billiard hall, saloons, a fishing tackle shop, a storage house, a news and book store, a drugstore, and a hardware store—as well as employers: a cabinetmaker and two cigar manufacturers. Beyond the train station, the South Foundry and

Machine Works (sometimes referred to as the South Florida Foundry and Machine Works) served as the city's first industrial manufacturer. By the 1920s, Central Avenue had replaced Church Street as the primary westward route, and by the 1930s, Robinson Street was taking a share of the traffic. In the 1950s, Colonial Drive was aligned to cross town in a straight line—a feat that could not be claimed by any of the earlier roadways—and to run clear across the state.

Though not on the original town plat map in 1875, Orange Avenue, which ended in an orange grove to the north and on the shore of Lake Lucerne to the south, quickly developed as the primary north-south artery in town. This view, looking north from Church Street, shows the growth that had taken place by 1884. Orange Avenue provided access to northeastern routes to Winter Park (and from there, Osceola/Lakeview, Oviedo, and Lake Jessup), Maitland, Longwood, Altamonte Springs, and Sanford; and northwestern routes to Forest City and Clay Springs/Wekiva, Apopka, Zellwood, Tavares, and Leesburg. Because of its importance, Orange Avenue was the first north-south street to be paved. It was surfaced with brick in 1907 from north of Oak Street (near the county jail) to the south side of Church Street. In 1914, it was also the first north-south roadway to be lighted.

In 1916, the Dixie Highway network was marked and paved through central Florida. Its route entered Orlando from the north and followed Edgewater Drive to Colonial to Orange Avenue, proceeded through the center of the city, circled the western side of Lake Lucerne to South Orange and South Main Streets, headed east on Gore Street, and finally went south on Kuhl Avenue. This network of improved existing roadways was the first federal effort to promote automobile travel between the North (as far as Canada) and the South and resulted in a wave of travelers known as "tin can tourists" to the sunny climate of Florida. The Orange Blossom Trail (OBT), or US-441, first replaced the Dixie Highway network and Orange Avenue in the 1930s. OBT, Interstate-4, Semoran Boulevard, and John Young Parkway are today's north-south routes that serve various parts of Orlando.

This view, looking north and northeast, probably from the San Juan Hotel, overlooks a sampling of the growth that was beginning to take place in that part of the young city by around 1892. While some settlement had begun, this quadrant was still considered country and few commercial establishments dared be so far from the center of town at Orange Avenue and Church Street. Some institutions were taking that big step, though, thanks to improvements such as straightening, destumping, and unrutting Orange Avenue and erecting boardwalks along a portion of the road. Among the permanent structures that had risen were the St. James Catholic Church (with the steeple) and the original Arcade Hotel (on the left of the photo, with the balconies) three blocks away at Robinson Street. The diagonal trail behind the corrals at the livery stable leads to St. Luke's Episcopal Church and the north shore of Lake Eola.

The northeast quadrant grew substantially while serving as the center of both city and county government for several decades, and the intersection of Orange Avenue and Central Avenue became the perceived center of Orlando. This perception arose primarily during Orlando's land boom of the early 1920s, when available land was developed into modern buildings—like the Angebilt Hotel (the redbrick building left of center) and the State Bank of Orlando and Trust Company Building (the redbrick structure on the right)—that towered above their older, established neighbors to the south without having to displace them. In addition, new residential areas became accessible as automobiles became more common. These areas were usually in former citrus groves to the north and east of the city's earlier centric development. The glass-and-steel building in the left foreground of this photograph is 20 North Orange, the site of the San Juan Hotel.

This view, looking west on Pine from Main Street, shows the rebuilding that took place after the 1884 Pine Street fire. The fire began between 4:00 a.m. and 5:00 a.m. on January 12 on the second floor of James Delaney's grocery building on the northwest corner of Pine and Main streets (in this photo, the store was in the vacant lot to the right). The fire spread quickly in the wooden building, but two clerks, who were sleeping at the time, awoke and escaped to warn the neighborhood. Next door (at the location of Taylor and Son Grocers, above), a milliner with the last name of Bassett and her children were safely rescued from a rear apartment. In the end, the grocery was a total loss, and the milliner lost her inventory of hats and the family's household goods; next door, on the northeast corner of Court Street, some of the stock in the drugstore of Dr. R. J. Gillham (who later joined the fire department) was saved.

In 1886, Delaney joined with builder Edward Kuhl to construct the Kuhl-Delaney Building (first building on the right) on the combined sites of the old Delaney grocery building and the *Reporter* building, which was located in a wooden structure on Main Street, behind the grocery. Norman Robinson's building (which had housed the millinery) was replaced at the same time. It had been built in 1884 with a veneered concrete finish that claimed to make it the first fireproof building in town. The Kuhl-Delaney Building opened with a new Delaney's Grocery and the Orlando Post Office (because Delaney was the postmaster). The Knights of Pythias Lodge made this their official hall in about 1922. In recent years, the building has assumed the name "The Phoenix." It houses some government and nonprofit offices.

Orlando's Lake Lucerne, shown here around 1904, was originally called Lake Lucindy, but it was renamed because someone thought it resembled the famous Swiss lake. James P. Hughey, a homesteader from Georgia, was the first to settle on the banks of Lake Lucerne. In 1855 or 1856, he built a log house on a low rise northwest of the lake. In 1881, the original Lucerne Hotel was built on the north bank, and two years later, the city approved extending Main Street to the lake and opening a new street to loop around the lake.

Homes sprang up quickly after that. Primarily, they were large homes, some of them small estates, that belonged to attorneys, affluent merchants, builders, and successful orange growers. In response, George Abbott organized the Lake Lucerne Improvement Society to lay a shell-paved walkway around the rim of the lake, to plant palms and magnolias on the sides of the walk, and to clay Lucerne Circle, the sandy road that looped the lake.

Lake Lucerne was the original home to Orlando's famous swans. Charles E. Lord brought the first two pairs—one pair white, one pair black—from England in 1910. At some point, the black swans were moved to Lake Eola. In 1956, a tree-lined causeway (visible on the far side of the water) opened through Lake Lucerne, connecting Orange Avenue north of the lake with Kuhl Avenue on the south—for the first time, Orlando had one continuous north-south roadway through the center of the city. Kuhl Avenue was renamed Orange Avenue in 1960. In the distance, beyond the causeway and the other side of the lake, are the two towers of the Kinneret Apartments. Lucerne Towers stands on the right of the walkway.

The park that surrounds Lake Eola (shown here between 1890 and 1906) has not always been the scenic oasis it is today. It was originally just called "the lake," or, if the water was low enough, "Sandy Beach" in the summer. The land was privately owned, though occasional swimmers and fishers were welcome visitors. Jacob Summerlin actually purchased the lake, and 200 acres of land around it, in the 1870s. In 1883, he gave a swath of land that followed the shoreline for use as a park. Supplemental lands, donated by John P.

Musselwhite (1909) and Eugene S. Sperry (1913), increased park space and improved access by adding room for roadways. Two years after Summerlin's initial gift, a temporary hall for exhibiting agricultural products was built; a racetrack followed two years later. These facilities were the start of the Orange County Fair and led to the larger fairgrounds and Exposition Park that was soon developed across town.

By the 1980s, land along the south, west, and north perimeter of the lake became prime commercial real estate. Fortunately, the shoreline immediately around the lake is protected with reversion rights to the original heirs (and public pressure on the city), should the land ever be considered for a purpose other than parkland. The first beautification efforts around the lake started in the mid-1910s with the installation of electric lights along the parkway, placement of the Sperry Fountain, and erection of the first bandstand. A lily pool, the wall of blooms (originally planted with sweet peas), an Oriental garden, a duck beach, a presentation area/outdoor chapel, and a scattering of benches followed over the years. Centennial Fountain, in the "middle" of the lake (it could not be placed in the exact center because of the lake's depth at that point), was first turned on in October 1957. Prominent buildings visible in this scene include the Waverly, Capital Plaza I and II, the Premiere Trade Center Towers, 20 North Orange, and the AmSouth Tower.

Lake Concord (right) and Lake Adair (right, background) are located only blocks from the current city center and just south and west of Lake Ivanhoe. This area (shown here in 1904) was not only a successful citrus grove but also the center of Orlando's one-time pineapple industry. George I. Russell had come to Orlando in 1885 and joined S. S. Waterhouse in his hay, grain, feed, and fertilizer business, the largest, in fact, of any in South Florida at the time.

After a while, he noticed that red pineapples grew in the yards of many homes in town and wondered why he couldn't grow them as a crop. He purchased land, built a home, and established his pinery. Before long, he was importing suckers of the finest varieties from Puerto Rico, Hawaii, and the Azores. He became so successful that his pineapple sheds covered several blocks in the area and he shipped boxcars full of pineapples to northern markets.

The area around Lakes Concord, Adair, and Ivanhoe that once showcased Orlando's agriculture-based heritage of citrus and pineapples now sports roadways and platted residences. Planning for this interstate began in 1953, and city leaders were eager to see it built through town. The route was to connect Daytona Beach and Tampa, but at the time Orlando was too small to influence the route's path through the middle of the state. After the state turnpike was adjusted east and north to be located nearer to Orlando, however, the business community succeeded in having the new interstate route moved, too. Construction for much of the highway's length began in late 1958, and the roadway opened in sections as completed. The last segment to open was this one, the bridge beside Lake Concord and over Lake Ivanhoe, which began carrying traffic in February 1965.

In 1886, at the time this photo was taken, few would argue that Grimm Family Groceries was not a "country" market. Though the city's mule-drawn trolley traveled one block farther before turning around, the site—on the west side of Orange Avenue, just north of Livingston (then sometimes called Livingstone)—was nearly five blocks north of the developed part of Orlando. Washington Grimm and his family had come from Winchester, Virginia, at the beginning of the decade. Like most area residents at this time, the Grimms lived above their place of work, though they did eventually move to a one-story addition and eventually into a separate house around the corner—also a typical progression as the town grew and families prospered. By the late 1910s, the Grimm Groceries building was gone. By the 1950s, the entire corner had become a used car lot.

The house next door to the grocery (in the historical photo) was built by T. W. "Tom" Mathews (variously referred to as T. J. Mathers, T. W. Mathers, or the same combination of initials with the surname spelled "Matthews," depending on the source), who was probably working at Luckie's lumber mill at this time. He later worked as an engineer at the Orlando Ice Company and eventually became one of Orlando's primary contractors and builders. He sold the home in 1889 to Olive B. Floyd, a traveling salesman for a wholesale grocery firm. Floyd planted grass and trees on the north side of Livingston all the way west to the railroad and built a water trough for animals. After many vacant years, some plans are being made for this block. Already partly visible on the back side is the new intracity bus station, which will also serve light-rail lines and a rapid transit system when they are built.

The Tremont Hotel (shown here soon after completion in the late 1890s) is one of the most interesting buildings Orlando has ever had. It was a combination of at least three structures—the 1875 frame courthouse; half of the Charleston House Hotel (the other half was also sold and became a rooming house known as Duke Hall); and part of a Methodist building, possibly the Union Free Church, which was torn down in 1893—all moved from other sites to the northeast corner of Main and Church streets. Inside, the hotel featured some of the original building's furnishings as well as articles that had been collected and imported from all over the world. Captain James Walle Wilmott had sailed around the world nine times before settling in Orlando in 1886 and piecing together his masterpiece. The hotel was razed in 1956 to make way for a parking lot. The property was purchased quickly, though, by the First Federal Savings and Loan Association.

The First Federal Savings and Loan Association started construction in the summer of 1962. Now called Magnolia Place, the structure has housed a variety of professional offices and seen service as a county office building. Before settling in Orlando, Captain Wilmott worked in the citrus industry near Geneva and Goldenrod. He then experimented with phosphate mining in Polk County. His first Orlando venture was in real estate—twenty-five acres east of the city—which proved quite successful. Not long after finishing his Tremont Hotel, the captain left again—to serve in the Spanish-American War. Before the Tremont Hotel was built, this location was the site of the county's second log courthouse in Orlando. Built in 1863 and burned during an 1868 trial, this two-story structure replaced the log cabin the county had adopted farther west on Church Street.

The Charles E. Johnson residence (shown here in 1885) was located on the northwest corner of Church Street and Liberty Avenue. Johnson had just arrived from Connecticut with E. Frank Sperry. Together, they founded the South Foundry and Machine Works, the city's first truly industrial venture, in 1886. Johnson served as the first vice president and superintendent. By 1894, the foundry was successful enough, and his family large enough, that Johnson built a large frame residence closer to town, on the northeast corner of Main Street and Jefferson, where he resided until at least April 1941, when the new federal building, courthouse, and post office opened across the street. Another partner, William C. Smith, built Orlando's first architect-designed house across from this one, on the southeast corner.

The site of the first Johnson home that was "so far out of town" is now part of the land under this parking structure. For thirty-one years, the South Foundry and Machine Works manufactured iron objects: pipes; fence pieces; building railings, columns, and other architectural details; railroad wheels; boiler grills; and made-to-order machined pieces. The plant suffered a disastrous fire in 1917, though, and all but the office building on the northwest corner of Pine Street and the railroad (Gertrude Street) was destroyed. In addition to his foundry activities, Johnson served the community as an alderman in 1889 and in 1911 became a vice president of the People's National Bank, which changed its name to First National Bank in 1920. When the new federal building, courthouse, and post office opened in 1941, an elderly Johnson strode across the street and "demanded" a tour of his new neighbor from the postmaster. Johnson's home was torn down in January 1949.

When Carrie Shaw heard that the Lakeview House (shown here around 1886) was available in 1894, she suggested to her aunt, the widow of her uncle Eban Shaw, that they try to manage it. Carrie had come to Orlando from Maine with her aunt when Mrs. Shaw returned from her husband's burial. As soon as Carrie arrived, she took a seamstress position with a dressmaker; she did such beautiful work that Edward W. Speir supported her in opening her own shop over his store at Pine Street and Main. At the age of seventeen, she had her own business and a number of employees. As the business grew, she needed more room and a more accessible space. Her aunt approved the move to Lakeview House, and in a few years, they were able to purchase it. Under their management, and later the management of Carrie and her husband Eugene S. Sperry, the Lakeview House became one of the most exclusive rooming houses in town.

Carrie and Eugene S. Sperry ran the Lakeview House (sometimes referred to as the Lakeview, or Lake View, Hotel) until 1916, when they sold the property. Before Carrie and her aunt became the owners, the house was owned by S. B. Harrington. Harrington became the first court reporter in the area when he arrived with his family in 1877. In 1878, he took over the *Orange County Reporter*, which he sold in 1880. He had also decided, in 1880, that he no longer wanted to run the Lakeview House, so he put it up for

lease. Eighty years later, in the summer of 1960, the University Club began construction of its own building on the site of the historic Lakeview House. The University Club was founded 1926 and met primarily in the Angebilt Hotel over the years. The organization is dedicated to supporting education by providing scholarship support to local colleges and universities. It is slated to move into a new development, to be built on the club's current site, in the next few years.

Located on Orange Avenue between Colonial and Concord, this home (shown here in August 1886) was built sometime in the 1880s, perhaps by Dr. Leo P. Lawrence (though some records list W. H. B. Lawrence as the owner). Lawrence came to Orlando from Tennessee in 1885 and opened a drugstore on the southwest corner of Orange Avenue and Pine Street. Inside, he had a "fountain," which was operated by Charles Guernsey for a time. The products of the fountain—or the never-ending rotation of young men hired to work it—drew quite a following over the years with younger crowds. The doctor moved to Tampa in 1906, but when he died, his widow Lucy Hayes Lawrence, who had originally come to Orlando in 1890, returned to serve as society editor for the *Reporter-Star* newspaper. The home was torn down in February 1923, along with several others, to make room for the Orange Court Hotel.

The Orange Court Hotel (not to be confused with the Orange Hotel, located on the west side of Court Street between Church Street and Pine, or the Hotel Orange) opened in March 1924. The Spanish Revival building was an apartment-hotel, which was common of the time. What was uncommon was that every unit—hotel included—had a private bath. Other accommodations included a sun parlor, an indoor swimming pool (one of the first in Orlando to be heated by steam), a ballroom, and several dining options. Outside was a tropical garden with five hundred varieties of tropical plants, shrubs, and flowers, as well as a small orange grove where guests could pick fruit when it was in season. The hotel was demolished in 1990. A recently announced apartment project for the block plans to incorporate the Spanish/Mediterranean style of the old hotel and will include some garden elements between buildings.

Until regular, scheduled service on the South Florida Railroad arrived on November 15, 1880, Orlando was a small scattering of wooden residences and necessary business structures halfway between the ports of Sanford and Kissimmee. Four stores, a hotel, a blacksmith and wagon shop, and a livery stable surrounded the county's adopted log courthouse on Church Street, less than one block east of the tracks. In the next few years, the area had expanded a block to the north along Orange Avenue and nearly three blocks to the east along Pine Street. Several rooming houses had opened and a reputable hotel, the Charleston House, had been built, as well as a few church buildings, a bank, a drugstore, a hardware store, a sawmill, and two more liveries. By the time the third depot (shown here in 1905) was dedicated in January 1890, the city's population had reached 2,856.

The railroad continued to influence the growth of Orlando. By 1886, the rails reached Tampa and traffic increased. Seven church buildings had been erected in those few more years, and two weekly newspapers were being published. The opera house, five "first-class" hotels, two carriage shops, an ice factory, four drugstores, and several restaurants were operating within an area that measured roughly eight blocks to the east and four blocks to the west of the train station (the city buildings had just opened on Oak Street, as had the new San Juan Hotel, so the city was only beginning to stretch northward). The Church Street Depot continued to serve rail passengers until 1927. In 1976, the building became one of Orlando's first listings on the National Register of Historic Places. Next to the station is a real (though cosmetically altered) 140-ton steam engine.

The Atlantic Coast Line (ACL) took over the South Florida Railroad (which was already one of the Plant System lines) in 1902 but did not change depots. The new Hughey Boulevard (later Sligh Boulevard) station was formally dedicated on January 11, 1927, with more than 6,000 people in attendance. The Spanish Mission Revival–style building was a welcome improvement at a time when the vast majority of people still traveled by train. In fact, Orlando was serviced by a second rail line from 1887 until

1967—the so-called Dinky Line (it was a narrow-gauge track), which eventually became part of the Seaboard system. The Dinky Line originally ran between Winter Park and Orlando but was extended to Oviedo by 1892 and by 1908 had connections to Savannah, Georgia, and points northward. In 1924, Seaboard opened a new station on the north side of Central Avenue to replace the Dinky Line's depot from the 1890s.

Not long after the new ACL station opened, the company announced three other construction projects for Orlando: transforming the Church Street Depot into a freight station, laying a second set of tracks through the city, and finishing the placement of electric safety signals at more than twenty crossings in the city. During the 1960s, the ACL and Seaboard Air Line Railroad agreed to merge, resulting in a combined company that was known as the Seaboard Coast Line Railroad. In 1980, the Seaboard Coast Line Railroad merged with the Chessie System to form CSX to continue handling the freight side of rail traffic. Amtrak had assumed the operation of nearly all intercity-passenger rail service in May 1971. Amtrak continues to serve Orlando at the Sligh Boulevard station with the Silver Meteor, the Silver Star, and the Sunset Limited.

Until the Great Depression, one of the favorite Orlando pastimes was putting on a parade. Parades were a public way to acknowledge building completions, business openings, and new equipment (like fire trucks); to celebrate successful crops and harvests; to install government officials; to recognize national and local holidays; to start and end the fair; to announce the circus; and to promote dignitaries and groups that were speaking or performing at the opera house or, later, the Municipal Auditorium. This February 14, 1914,

parade was held to make a point, with groups marching to promote the issue of women's voting rights. It had been organized by the Orlando Suffrage League, which sprang up in 1913 along with the Florida Equal Suffrage Association, both led by the Unitarian church's Reverend Mary Safford, a national leader in the suffrage movement. Perhaps as a result, the Men's Equal Suffrage League was formed in March.

On April 25, 1917, just a few weeks after war was declared on Germany to bring the United States into World War I, Orlando held one of its largest-ever parades. According to accounts, all stores, businesses, and schools closed at 4:30 p.m. At 5:00, Confederate veteran Benjamin M. Robinson led off atop a gray hose named Frances. Other pioneer residents followed, ahead of bands, floats, and decorated cars in support of Company C, First Florida Regiment. That evening, the Lucerne Theater hosted patriotic addresses by Unitarian minister Mary Safford, Newton P. Yowell for the Red Cross, J. H. Sadler for local farmers, and Sexton Johnson, who read President Woodrow Wilson's declaration of war. The Pledge of Allegiance and a variety of patriotic songs ended the somber event. One of the more joyous "just because" parades was the Pajama Parade on August 20, 1929. Fewer parades are held these days. Prominent buildings that can be seen in this view include the Premiere Trade Center Towers (left) and CNL Tower at City Commons (straight ahead).

When the San Juan de Ulloa Hotel was built in 1885, no one could have foreseen the changes it would encounter. Orlando's citizenry thought the builder was crazy—at the time, Orlando's population was only 2,000, and the entire central business district was basically three blocks by two blocks in area. The San Juan (shown here around 1917) was, by far, the largest building in town; it was also one of the largest hotels many of Orlando's residents had ever seen. Henry S. Kedney was not discouraged, though. He had come from Minnesota to settle in Maitland in 1870, then moved into Orlando in 1885. He started planning and building the original three-story hotel almost immediately. Although he had been successful, Kedney decided to move on in 1893 to pursue other interests and sold the property to Harry L. Beeman. Before long, Beeman had added two more floors and a veranda on the Central Avenue side that grew into a favorite meeting and gathering place.

In 1922, the San Juan expanded to keep its competitive edge over the brand-new Angebilt Hotel that was being built across the street. In 1955, another upgrade and reconfiguration added space for business meetings and a ballroom on the mezzanine level. The San Juan first experienced hard times in the 1960s. It was closed in 1975 and demolished in 1980 and 1981. This diagonally situated, sixteen-story office building was finished in 1983.

It is currently referred to by its address, 20 North Orange. By surviving ninety-six years, the San Juan outlasted all of its late-nineteenth century contemporaries: the Tremont Hotel, the Hotel Wyoming, and the Lucerne Hotel all fell before the San Juan. Even the newer, flashier Angebilt Hotel ceased being a hotel in a shorter length of time.

Gordon Rogers arrived in Orlando in 1886 and proceeded to build a structure that, even then, was considered beautiful. Finished in heavily embossed zinc panels from England (which were also used on the ceilings inside), the building housed a liquor store on the ground floor (opened in 1887). From its beginnings, the Rogers Building, shown here between 1906 and 1910, was a meeting place for British immigrants. Men gathered in a first-floor pub to drink ales, smoke, and play cards. The women used a second entrance to reach the upstairs ballroom, where they could socialize. Dances and theater productions were also offered there. A significant number of early Orlando residents had come from Britain in the 1880s—retirees seeking a milder climate, young men who were not in line to inherit their family's properties or fortunes in England, and general laborers. These English folks brought their loves of tennis, croquet, golf, and polo to a rather unrefined area.

Placed on the National Register of Historic Places in 1983, the building, inside and out, stands much as it did in 1910. Over the years, the former liquor store and social club has housed a grocery store, a church, a newspaper, a dance studio, and many restaurants. The Rogers Building was recently renovated again and is currently used as the University of Central Florida's Downtown Media Arts Center, or DMAC, a public screening room for independent and locally produced films and media programs. During that renovation, it was discovered that the building's original exterior may have been a stucco made of rock-hard plaster laced with horsehair applied to a metal lath. Such a finish would have appeased a new city ordinance that required all structures downtown to be built of fireproof masonry. That ordinance was passed after a fire swept through some Pine Street businesses in 1884, two years before Gordon Rogers arrived.

Charles and Gilbert Lee opened a hardware store on this site in 1884, which was known for a time as Ogilvie Hardware. Tenants of this building (shown here in 1923) included the W. R. Link Tire Company and the Potter Candy Company. The Potter Candy Company, established in 1922, made candies under the brand name "Orlando-Maid." These candies were so popular across the state that a new factory had to be built in May 1925 to increase production. When Potter was forced to move his retail store for construction of the new ten-story State Bank of Orlando building, he moved across the street into the newly opened San Juan Hotel addition. He moved back into the Central Avenue side of the new tower in the fall of 1925. Potter lived in a home at the southeast corner of Fern Creek Avenue and Robinson Street, on a twenty-acre citrus grove. One of his sons, Thomas G. Lee, would later establish the T. G. Lee Dairy on that property.

The city's banks had not had an easy time in the late 1800s or early 1900s. The first official bank, the Bank of Orlando, was established in late 1883 but was forced to reorganize in February 1886, when it became the First National Bank of Orlando. Citizens National Bank, which opened in August 1887, merged with the First National Bank of Orlando and became the largest bank of the time in central Florida before it failed following the national financial panic of 1893 and the area's twin freezes in December 1894 and February 1895.

Seemingly with better luck, the State Bank of Orlando and Trust Company had become so successful by 1920 that it opened this new building at 1 North Orange Avenue in 1924. Five years later, however, on Monday, August 6, 1929, the State Bank of Orlando and Trust Company failed to open. The Florida Bank at Orlando reopened in its place on March 10, 1930. The building now provides office space. Until their new structure opened recently, the first floor housed the law library of the Florida A&M University College of Law.

In 1883, Nathaniel Poyntz opened the only bank in the central Florida region—the Bank of Orlando. A year later, it was reorganized to become the First National Bank, which was moved shortly thereafter to the first floor of the newly constructed, brick Joy Building (shown here ca. 1914–1916), at the northeast corner of Orange Avenue and Pine Street. The first floor served as the bank offices; a legal firm, Hammond and Johnson, was on the second floor. The Joy Building was one of the first structures built after a January 1884 fire that destroyed part of the city's first generation of wood buildings. The fire started before dawn in James Delaney's grocery on the northwest corner of Pine and Main streets. It spread quickly westward and northward but destroyed only four businesses, thanks to a rain the previous night and a quick response by citizens and the volunteer fire department.

Citrus baron Dr. Philip Phillips announced plans for a $50,000 theater in September 1916 that would replace the 1885 Joy Building and both of the smaller wooden buildings (which had sand foundations) on either side of it. The theater actually cost $100,000 before opening on October 10, 1917—a foreboding signal of future financial problems. Its opening film was *Wild and Wooly*, starring Douglas Fairbanks. By early October 1929, the Phillips Theater had closed and reopened as the Ritz, complete with a new flashing neon marquee. The film that night was John Gilbert in *His Glorious Night*. The Great Depression, which was hard on movie houses citywide, brought an end to the theater in the summer of 1934. A second floor was then added to provide room for shops and offices. The building served as a W. T. Grant's store for many years. It currently provides studio and gallery space for artists on the first floor as well as an open second-floor reception space.

The Charleston House (inset; shown ca. 1886–1888) was originally called the Lucky House, after its builder H. A. Luckie of Charleston, South Carolina. When the thirty-room hotel opened on New Year's Night 1882, it was the best in town, and largest—until the San Juan opened in 1885. The elaborate porches and balconies were not original but were added within a few years. Historians credit the Charleston House with "pulling" the center of town to the north. When the hotel was dismantled in the 1890s, a portion of the building was moved and incorporated into J. W. Wilmott's Tremont Hotel. By that time, the citizens of Orlando had become so attached to the Charleston House that when the T. J. Watkins Block (shown in the late 1930s) was built in 1895, it was often called the Charleston Block. The new building housed a variety of stores and offices over the years but slowly gave way to the needs of one tenant: McCrory's.

The J. G. McCrory Stores Corporation (McCrory's) first rented space in the Watkins Block in 1908 for a small retail shop and its office. As the chain grew, a regional office opened. Over the years, additional space was needed for the expanding regional office and for a larger retail area. In 1941, the Moorish dome was removed and an extensive remodeling and new construction project took place to upgrade the office space and to open the entire first floor for retail. McCrory's closed in 1989. After years of attempting to save the historic block, it was demolished in December 2003 and January 2004. In its place has risen the Premiere Trade Center Towers. The structure consists of a thirteen-story office condominium tower, a seventeen-story office condominium tower; a twelve-screen movie theater; retail space; a 305-unit, twenty-seven-story residential condo tower; and a 1,500-space parking garage.

Orlando's first traffic lights were "installed" in January 1924—but they were far from mechanized or automatic. When traffic was congested and a signal was needed at an intersection, a patrolman was assigned to illuminate and control a lantern-topped pole. The lantern had red lenses on two opposite sides and green lenses on the other two opposing sides. The poles were positioned into concrete pedestals in the middle of the intersection and rotated as needed until the traffic cleared. Perhaps surprisingly, this system lasted until June 1925, when city voters approved appropriating funds for overhead, suspended signal lights. In November 1929, the signal tower at the intersection of Orange Avenue and Central (shown here in 1927) was outfitted with loudspeakers for music, presumably Christmas music.

The signal tower at the intersection was not removed until September 1937. It had served no purpose (other than to hold signs advertising store sales and community events, like ball games at Tinker Field) since 1925, when Mayor James L. Giles had mounted it to flip a switch that turned on the new overhead signal system. The city's first light posts (two are visible in the previous photo—one under the clock; another on the opposite side of Orange Avenue) were designed by Guy R. Ramsey, a city engineer, and installed in 1914. They were octagonal with smooth edges and made of white cement. The earliest such lamps were erected in the business district and around Lake Lucerne. Until a few years ago, the signal tower's absence would have been the only major difference in this view. Now, with construction of the Premiere Trade Center Towers, a building difference is noticeable, too.

Historians say that baseball has been played on the site of Tinker Field since 1914, but a formal ballpark was not built until 1923. The diamond's opening game was held on April 19, between the Orlando Bulldogs and the Lakeland Highlanders. With nearly all the businesses in town closed for the game, more than 1,700 fans turned out—Orlando won, 3–1. The original 1,500-seat stadium was named after Joe Tinker, who moved to Orlando following a major league career (most of it as shortstop with the Chicago Cubs) that began in 1902. Over the years, Tinker Field hosted spring training for many major-league teams (primarily the Cincinnati Reds, Brooklyn Dodgers, Washington Senators, and Minnesota Twins) and served as the home diamond for several Florida state and southern league teams. The ballpark was remodeled in 1963 with the addition of a concessions concourse and improved field lighting and fan seating.

Tinker Field was placed on the National Register of Historic Places in May 2004. Its overshadowing neighbor, the Citrus Bowl (on the right), was built in 1936 as the Orlando Stadium. When the stadium began hosting the Tangerine Bowl in 1947, the stadium itself became known as the Tangerine Bowl; in 1983, the annual game changed its name to the Citrus Bowl, and the stadium again followed suit. The stadium has undergone renovations and additions over the years that have increased its number of seats to 70,000. Of interest to followers of television trivia, the Citrus Bowl was the home of the imaginary Breakers, from the series *Coach*, between 1995 and 1997. Now separated from the center of town by an interstate highway and other obstacles, Tinker Field no longer sees the action it once did, but popularity among ballpark enthusiasts remains high, and the facility stands at the ready.

Oak Street was named for a grove of live oak trees that once graced its border. At one time, this street ran east from Orange Avenue, across Court Street, across Main Street, and into the middle of a block where it would have met up with Magnolia Avenue had the Summerlin Hotel not blocked that street at Washington. Its length was shortened with the construction of the 1892 courthouse to run only from Orange Avenue to Court Street; the eastern portion was realigned and renamed Summerlin Place. The north side of Oak (the right side in this photo) was once the center of city government; the 1885 brick city hall buildings, jail, bell tower, and fire station were all located there. Part of the old city hall eventually became John Cook's automotive garage, later served as the Florida Motor Lines (intercity) depot, and even later became the Orlando Rapid Transit Company (intracity) depot. Beyond these buildings, on the corner lot with Orange, was the first home of the Rosalind Club and later the Board of Trade. The Angebilt Hotel rose there in 1923.

Along the south side of Oak Street (the left side of the photo), the Charles Rock Bakery stood on Orange Avenue for nearly twenty years after Rock bought the building in 1900. This was actually his third location, and the citizens of Orlando thought he was crazy to move so far away from Pine Street and the commercial district of town. The smell of fresh bread, though, managed to bring his customers north to the government center. Buck Bass's house stood about halfway down the block. Built in 1878, the house gained fame in 1915 when it was recognized as the oldest standing landmark in the city. Some citizens suggested it should have beeen moved to the west side of Lake Eola and used as a museum, but without funding, the project died. Two years later, the house was condemned and torn down. On the near end of the street, after the Bass House was demolished, a new county jail was built in 1917. The old abstract office had stood on the very corner. Oak Street was renamed Wall Street in 1924. It is now a short pedestrian mall known as Wall Street Plaza and has restaurants with outdoor seating lining both sides. Offices are housed in the higher floors of most buildings, including the Angebilt Building and 20 North Orange (ahead).

Promotional materials for the Jefferson Court Hotel buildings (two identical buildings separated by an alleyway; shown here in 1937) boasted that they provided "the utmost in service and hospitality." The hotel buildings were completed in 1918, a year after the E-shaped Jefferson Court Apartments, which were separated from the hotel units by a parklike garden of citrus trees and decorative plantings. Some of the apartments were furnished with refrigerators, kitchenettes with gas ranges and ovens, and bedroom sets. The exciting new project was financed by the Orlando Investment Company, a consortium of twenty-five local businessmen—nearly every prominent name in Orlando at the time, including L. L. Payne, Eugene Duckworth, H. H. Dickson, John Ange, Harry Beeman, J. M. Cheney, C. D. Christ, Harry P. Leu, John McEwan, and Philip Phillips.

The Jefferson Court Hotel and Apartments complex was torn down in the summer of 1954. The Haas Building was later built on the property and became home to the downtown J. C. Penney's store in 1960, when it was moved from its original location on West Church Street, where it had been since opening in 1940. Penney's closed in 1985, and the building housed a series of business occupants and government agencies. The building, now the UHB Building, recently underwent a massive renovation project that included the addition of two floors. This photo also helps place into context the buildings of Orange Avenue from the north. Beyond UHB, the visible structures are 20 North Orange (site of the San Juan Hotel), the historic Dickson-Ives Building, and the CNL Center Tower at City Commons, which is straight ahead. On the left, the AmSouth Tower and the Angebilt Building are visible.

This is a photograph that would never have been available except for the fact that it was kept in an accident file from 1938. In the first half of the twentieth century, many central Florida locations looked just like this shot—desolate except for an occasional dirt road, a scattering of farmhouses, and acre after acre of orange groves. This particular location is situated only one block off Orange Avenue, at this time the only direct road between Orlando and Winter Park. The spot is roughly three miles from the center of each town. Residential development had been planned for this area in the 1920s, but shortages in building supplies, a killer hurricane in September 1926, and finally the stock market crash in 1929 and the Great Depression snowballed to detour those plans. The City of Orlando collected or purchased parcels throughout the 1930s as lenders foreclosed on the properties.

Today, Princeton Avenue is a major east-west corridor that connects all of the primary north-south routes: Mills Avenue–U.S. 17/92; Orange Avenue, Interstate 4, Edgewater Avenue, Orange Blossom Trail, and John Young Parkway. Instead of the grove that used to stand here, the Orlando Science Center (OSC) and CineDome Planetarium can be seen ahead. The OSC sits at the southwest corner of Loch Haven Park, a rolling green space that resulted from the collection of foreclosed and defaulted development properties during the 1930s. Also in the park are the Orlando Museum of Art, the Mennello Museum of American Art, the Civic Theaters of Central Florida, the Orlando-UCF Shakespeare Festival theaters, the Orlando Philharmonic Orchestra, and the Orlando Garden Club.

The Union Free Church provided the first space for public education in the city. By 1884, the city had 292 registered pupils and was forced to move three grades into donated space on the first floor of the Masonic Lodge. In 1886, the city took over a wooden structure that had been built by the Methodist Episcopal Church as an academy. In addition, a school for black students was opened in 1886 at the corner of Garland and Church streets. When the academy building, on Jackson Street between Orange Avenue and Boone Street, burned in 1905, a brick structure replaced it the following year. That was the Orlando Public School (which became City Hall in 1926). The West Central Elementary School (shown here in the 1930s) was built in 1916 at a time when education was finally expanding.

The Orange County Department of Health moved into the old West Central Elementary School building in 1957. In January 1973, a predawn fire swept through the facility. It was demolished shortly thereafter, and this new building was erected on the back of the lot. Central Florida has not always been known for its healthy environment and restorative attributes. When soldiers were fighting the Seminoles in the mid-1800s, they rarely moved from July to September because of humid heat, pounding rains, and swamp diseases—like dysentery and fevers—that were, many times, deadly. Mosquitoes, fleas, and flies were rampant as well. The health department helped improve and maintain central Florida's unpleasantries for its growing population.

In 1900, Leslie Pell-Clarke donated his home near St. Luke's Episcopal Church to be used by the church's bishop, William Crane Gray (the home was thereafter commonly called the "Bishopstead"). When Gray moved out of his quarters, the former home at Central and Liberty streets was converted into the Cathedral School (shown here ca. 1930), which opened its doors later that year. The school was originally named for Pell-Clarke, who had made the transaction possible. Over the years, the Cathedral School served as a regular school for local girls, a regular school for both boys and girls, and a residential school for boys and girls that attracted students from nearly every state in the country. In 1905, a second building was built, and in 1906, a third. In 1917, a neighboring residence was added to the campus. A final hall was erected in 1929. Interestingly, the private school was one of the first to desegregate. It closed in 1967 and was demolished.

The Capital Plaza I tower was completed in 1980. Based on the southern shore of Lake Eola, the Embassy Suites Downtown hotel opened in the late 1990s, along with Capital Plaza II. The Sperry Fountain was donated by E. Frank Sperry in 1913. The central figure is a wrought-iron bittern, reminiscent of the egrets, herons, and swans that visit the two downtown lakes, Eola and Lucerne, or call them home. Sperry served as mayor from 1913 to 1916, when he became the second Orlando mayor to die in office. He had arrived in 1885 from Connecticut and was a member of the so-called English Colony and cofounder of the South Foundry and Machine Works. He was first elected to the city council in 1892, though he had earlier served as an alderman, and he served on the city's first park board, whose initial assignment was to lay sidewalks around Lake Eola.

The first stream of Orlando-bound tourists was already arriving before the turn of the 1900s. By that time, the city had several hotels located around town, but some travelers preferred to have smaller, more traditional quarters with a more comfortable, or homey, atmosphere. For them, "tourist houses" were perfect. Tourist houses were often run by lonely widows who had extra rooms to let. They usually charged a small room rate and allowed (or encouraged) their visitors to take meals around a table, relax on the porch, and visit with them—similar to today's smaller bed-and-breakfasts. With Orange Avenue as the earliest north-south route through town, it was natural that this bend in the road, which was the last before heading around Lake Lucerne and out of town or the first upon entering town, became a hotbed of such facilities.

By the 1950s, an array of north-south routes went around the center of Orlando, and few travelers came through the center of town; fewer needed room or board. Now that two interstate superhighways carry drivers "above" town, that is even more true. Instead, the space is today home to an assortment of commercial offices and government buildings, like the Orlando Utilities Commission and City Commons (both out of the photo, to the left). A performing arts center is planned for the blocks on the right (also out of

the photo). The multiwindowed building in the historic photo is not the same building seen in this photo. The historic building was built as the I. W. Phillips Dodge Agency, an automobile dealership with a parking garage, in 1923 or 1924. It was also known as the Exchange Building and the American Building before being demolished in the 1990s. The structure in the current photo is the Grand Bohemian Hotel.

The building that housed Rutland's Men's Clothing Store for many years (shown here in the 1940s) was erected by Joseph P. Rutland, who purchased the property from Lawrence Lawton in the middle of 1940. At the time, the parcel included a gas station, a parking lot, and a cabstand. The two-story men's store was built in 1942. The architect for the project was Floyd Earl DeLoe, who also designed the Reeves Terrace Housing Project and was the first president of the Mid-Florida Chapter of the American Institute of Architects. Rutland's closed this downtown location in the late 1960s but remained open in the suburban Colonial Plaza Shopping Center at Colonial and Bumby. In 1948, Rutland was one of the small group of businessmen who helped found the Orlando Union Rescue Mission.

Three floors were added in 1952 with a surprisingly faithful adherence to the Art Moderne lines of the original. The Rutland's building is now home to several professional offices and Century Bank. Before the gas station, parking lot, and cabstand that Joseph Rutland bought, the St. Charles Hotel occupied this site. The St. Charles was originally the home of R. L. Harris, who, at the turn of the 1900s, established the tuberculosis sanitarium on Lake Estelle that evolved into Florida Hospital. He was also credited with having the first automobile in Orlando. Harris sold the property at Orange Avenue and Washington Street to Mrs. Charles I. Hilpert and her aunt Louise Faul in 1908. They converted the property and ran the hotel until 1925. Much of the St. Charles Hotel was torn down in July 1928. The Angebilt Hotel, in the background, was converted to offices and office suites in 1988.

When Florida became a state, no daily newspapers existed, even in the established towns of Jacksonville, Tallahassee, St. Augustine, and Key West. Orlando's first paper started a year after incorporation: the *Orange County Reporter*. The paper changed hands frequently and names occasionally, but it stayed in production into modern times. The *Sentinel-Star* (whose plant is shown here, to the right, ca. 1958) and today's *Orlando Sentinel* are descendants of that paper. The *Sentinel-Star* was created on January 22, 1931, with the merger of the *Orlando Morning Sentinel* and the *Evening Reporter-Star*. One Sunday edition was printed. Both papers were then published from the Fraternal Building on the west side of South Orange Avenue, between Church and Jackson streets. The *Morning Sentinel* had been moved here from the Magruder Arcade in October 1916.

The main tower of the SunTrust Center Complex is currently the tallest building in Orlando, at thirty floors and 441 feet. Construction ended in 1988. The previous building on the site was the First National Bank of Orlando headquarters, which opened in March 1960 after the earlier buildings, including the Orland Hotel, the City Luggage and Jewelry Company store, the *Sentinel-Star* Building (the combined *Sentinel-Star* had moved to a new plant on North Orange Avenue in August 1951), and the old Montgomery Ward, were razed in 1956. In 1985, the First National Bank of Orlando merged with the Trust Company of Georgia to create the corporate structure for SunTrust Banks. The Orlando bank used the name Sun First National Bank until 1995, when it adopted the SunTrust name. The fourteen-story 1960 building, made of granite, marble, and glass, was demolished for this first building of the SunTrust Center Complex, the actual bank tower.

Before Orange County built an official courthouse in 1863, it conducted county business in a two-room log cabin that stood close to where the Hotel Martin (shown here in the 1950s) once stood, just east of the railroad station on the south side of Church Street. The county used the room closest to town; religious groups and the first school classes shared the building, using the west room. In 1883, Dr. James Nixon Butt arrived from North Carolina and built a two-story brick building that housed his office and drugstore, as well as a sundries shop. When he moved to another office on Orange Avenue, Dr. James Horace Smith from Georgia took over the building. It also served the N. P. Nemo Dry Goods Store, Campbell's Pumps & Wells, and a restaurant. By 1919, a third floor had apparently been added to Butt's building and the neighboring brick structures had been built. All three were operating as hotels at the time.

A revitalization effort of this area began in 1973 when the Church Street Station Partnership agreed to renovate and remodel the historic two-block section rather than demolish and rebuild. Later redevelopment efforts were not as dedicated to preservation, and several buildings had been demolished by 2005. This courtyard and set of shops now line the entrance to part of the Church Street Market shopping complex and the rear of the SunTrust Center Complex (visible in the background). In Orlando's early decades, Church Street was the primary route for entering and exiting west Orlando. Because it was the major road, it saw most of the first development west from Orange Avenue: the first sidewalks in 1883, the first brick streets in 1907, and the first asphalt-paved streets after the bricks were coated.

The towering 1922 addition to the San Juan Hotel (shown here in 1938) was an effort to modernize the San Juan's image and to maintain its position as *the* hotel in Orlando. The eight floors also enabled the hotel to add much-needed space. The year before ground was broken for the addition, Braxton Beacham had bought the old county jail and torn it down to build the Beacham Theatre. When the Beacham opened on December 9, 1921, it was the grandest of the many theaters in town at the time. It had seating for 1,200 and boasted of being "constructed entirely of concrete" and therefore fireproof. It was not one of the famed movie palaces, but its red curtain, balcony, flowered carpeting, and air-conditioning drew crowds for nearly fifty years.

The Beacham Theatre closed its long run as a movie house in 1975. Its stage continued to be used for musical acts until the late 1980s as the Great Southern Music Hall. The house is currently used as a nightclub, which is a better fate than its neighbor—the San Juan was demolished in 1981.

Edward B. Hess, whose home is pictured here, was at least partly responsible for refining typewriters to the point where a typist could see what was being typed—the "ultimate visible type writer." Hess's accomplishments also helped enable an upright arrangement of the mechanism, creating the look that became standard into the 1960s and allowed the introduction of "portable," though quite weighty, models. Hess kept patenting improvements, and by 1923, he was reported to have obtained more than 140 typewriter-related patents. He and his wife, Eliza, moved to Orlando and into this home—one of the first in the Marks Street neighborhood northeast of the central part of the city—in 1928.

The Hess home contains several features of a regional architectural style known as Florida Mediterranean Revival. Stucco siding, flat roofs, arched window frames, arcaded entryways, iron window grills, and iron faux balconies are hallmarks of the style. The style was commonly used in central and southeastern parts of the state between 1915 and 1940. The home remains a private residence.

Bishop John Moore bought an entire block of property (bounded by Orange, Main, Robinson, and Jefferson) for the Catholic parish in 1881, but a building for mass was not started until 1885. That was when Father Felix P. Swemberg authorized construction of this first building (shown here as it appeared in about 1900) in the middle of the block along Orange Avenue. In 1889, a convent was erected on the Main Street side of the property to house a few members of the Sisters of St. Joseph, who came to Orlando from St.

Augustine to start and operate a parochial school on the property. St. Joseph's Academy was immediately successful with an initial enrollment of thirty students. By 1927, the school boasted an enrollment of two hundred students and a teaching staff of seven sisters. The academy moved into larger quarters north of Lake Eola on Ridgewood Avenue in 1929, and changed its name to St. James School.

Now known as St. James Catholic Cathedral, the sanctuary, offices, and a courtyard take up the entire frontage along Orange Avenue. This complex was dedicated in March 1952. The side of the block that made up St. Joseph's convent and the academy the sisters ran was sold to the United States government in 1939 for use as the area's new federal courthouse, office building, and post office. The Sisters of St. Joseph continued to make up the teaching staff of St. James School until 1973, when the change to nonparochial status began. In November 1977, St. James School was officially dedicated as the Cathedral School of St. James and opened to any local elementary-level student. As part of a recent renovation of the federal building, a portion of that building was designated for use by the Catholic Diocese so its chancery offices in the downtown area could be consolidated.

For the first few years of the group's existence, members of the Episcopal faith alternated Sunday services at the Union Free Church with the Baptist and Methodist congregations. Those early services were likely led by Francis Eppes, a grandson of Thomas Jefferson, who also held services in his home on the west side of Lake Pinelock, perhaps as early as 1867, when he arrived with his family. Eppes read scriptures daily in Latin and Greek and discussed their meanings with anyone who would listen. He worked tirelessly to establish the Episcopal church in Orlando but died in 1881, one year before the first portion of this building (shown ca. 1900) was erected on the southwest corner of Main and Jefferson streets. It was enlarged in 1884, when the name St. Luke's Parish was adopted, a second time in 1893 with the addition of the bell tower, and a third time in 1902. In 1922, this structure was moved south on the lot to make room for a new Gothic Revival–style cathedral.

Dedicated on Easter Sunday in April 1926, St. Luke's Cathedral opened with seating for seven hundred worshippers and an exceptional collection of stained glass. But, with shortages in building supplies and economic problems, parts of the building were only "temporarily" finished. Recovery from a major hurricane in September 1926 and the stock market crash in 1929 further delayed completion. Surprisingly, the bell tower and chapel were completed in 1933, during the Great Depression. But not until a renovation in the early 1970s was the wall of the nave finished, along with erection of a choir gallery and installation of an eighty-eight-rank pipe organ. And, not until work in 1986 and 1987 was the last temporary wall from 1926 removed. After sixty years, St. Luke's Cathedral was finally completed, much as it had been originally planned. The older building, which had eventually been used for church offices, was razed in 1940 to make room for an education wing.

Christian Scientists began holding lectures in Orlando in 1917, when they met at the Lucerne Theater. The Lucerne, on the east side of Court Street, between Church Street and Pine Street, was a relatively new auditorium (opened in December 1911) that featured a balcony and seating on an elevated floor. By 1926, the Christian Scientists had decided to build their own space. George Foote Dunham, a Christian Scientist and architect of some fifty churches, designed the structure pictured above, which opened in May 1928. The interior is two-and-a-half stories tall; the masonry exterior features a prominent copper dome. Oddly, though this location on Rosalind Avenue was only two blocks east of Orange Avenue (the main north-south street in town) and facing Lake Eola, it had never been developed. In fact, much of the land along this stretch was not even divided into lots until sometime between 1908 and 1913.

During the mid-1970s, the Christian Scientists moved to a new building on Fern Creek Avenue. In 1975, their old building was purchased by the St. George Greek Orthodox Church. In June 1980, it was placed on the National Register of Historic Places. The land in this block was once part of Jacob Summerlin's in-town home. Summerlin's holdings in early Florida once included rangeland along the Caloosahatchee River and lands that have grown into Lake City (through his father's estate) and Bartow. In 1873, he brought his family to Orlando, where, the next year, he built a large home at the head of Magnolia Avenue, facing the corner of Main Street and Washington. He also bought two hundred acres around and including Lake Eola; its western boundary was West Street, which later became Rosalind Avenue—the roadway that runs in front of this building.

The Union Free Church, built in 1872, once stood on part of this block—150 feet south of Pine Street and 100 feet east of Main. The Union Free Church provided a meeting space on alternating Sundays for all the religious denominations in town at the time. It also served as the public schoolhouse during the week, relieving the log courthouse on Church Street of both duties. Baptists in Orlando were meeting in private homes by 1858 but allegedly disbanded during the Civil War. They reorganized in 1871 as the Bethel Baptist Church and met at the Union Free Church before constructing their own sanctuary on the northwest corner of Pine Street and Garland Avenue in 1882. The group moved back to Pine and Main in 1897, after the other denominations had built elsewhere, and into their new home (inset). The newer, larger edifice was dedicated in May 1915.

The 1915 building was demolished in 1975 (the congregation had built another sanctuary in 1955; it is visible at the far left) to make room for this six-story structure, whose ground floor tenants include the Mad Cow Theatre. The Mad Cow is a professional theater company that presents both classic and contemporary plays—the best of American and world literature—for a wide range of audiences. The Mad Cow has also been recognized for its educational program of original works that are designed for students and young audiences.

Members of the Presbyterian faith organized in 1876 and alternated Sundays with the three original groups that met in the Union Free Church. They then moved into a series of temporary structures on the northeast corner of Central Avenue and the railroad tracks. In January 1889, fire claimed the last of these, and the group met in the courthouse and the Opera House until a frame sanctuary was erected at the southeast corner of Church and Main streets. In 1902, a small and dwindling group of Congregationalists merged with the Presbyterian group, and the Congregational Church building was moved to the Presbyterian grounds. That building was used until this dignified structure hosted its first service on December 27, 1914. Designed by architect Murray S. King, the new sanctuary featured stained-glass windows made by the Jacoby Art Glass Company in St. Louis. King also designed the Angebilt Hotel, the Wyoming Hotel's 1923 three-story addition, and the Wescott/Beardall residence, as well as a number of other commercial buildings of the time. After 1914, the old Congregational Church building was used as a Sunday school and lecture room.

The Presbyterian faith was perhaps the most popular denomination in Orlando, and many churches formed in different outlying areas after the turn of the century. After struggling for so many years, the central church itself kept growing, as well. A three-story Bible school and education building was built about halfway down the Church Street block, at Palmetto, in 1926. Groundbreaking ceremonies for a larger sanctuary took place on April 18, 1954, toward the opposite end of the Church Street block. Newton P. Yowell, a cofounder of the Yowell-Duckworth Company department store and the oldest active member of the church, turned over the first shovel of dirt. At the time it was erected, the 142-foot steeple of the new structure was the tallest object in town. The cornerstone of this corner building, Yowell Hall, was laid in 1958.

In the mid-1910s, a small building formerly used by the Seventh-Day Adventist Church on the southeast corner of Terry Street and Central Avenue was purchased for use by Orlando's small Jewish population. This would be the first dedicated temple for the local group. Before long, though, just a block away in the home of Harry Kanner, an immigrant from Husi, Romania, plans were being made to build a larger place of worship. The result was this building in 1926: Congregation Ohev Shalom temple and school.

Located on the northwest corner of Church Street and Eola Drive, the synagogue was in the midst of the city's new, fast-growing residential area to the south of Lake Eola, six blocks east of the county courthouse. The building served until 1974, when a new temple was dedicated on Goddard Avenue, northwest of the downtown area. Now with seven hundred families, Congregation Ohev Shalom has voted to acquire land on Maitland Avenue for a new facility.

Congregation Ohev Shalom synagogue, once on Florida's Jewish Heritage Trail, was torn down in late 2002 to make room for the high-rise condominium that adjoins this parking garage—the Sanctuary. Israel and Rose Shader had arrived in Orlando from Pittsburgh in 1913 to join their friends and in-laws, Peter and Bella Wittenstein, who had come a year earlier. The two families settled near each other on the western side of Lake Fairview—one family opened the Fairvilla Dairy; the other bought an orange grove. Moses Levy, the patriarch of another family of orange farmers who had also come from Pittsburgh, kept the area's sole Torah at his home, which also served as the gathering place for holy day ceremonies. All three were early supporters of starting a synagogue in Orlando. In the mid-1910s, their dreams began to take shape.

Only months before Florida became a state in March 1845, the name of Mosquito County was changed to Orange County. At the time, its area consisted of the majority of the east coast and the central interior, from about present-day Ormond Beach and Ocala south to the shores of Lake Okeechobee and including a strip west from there to Charlotte Harbor on the coast of the Gulf of Mexico. Because of the area's immense size, its varying population-growth patterns, and activity associated with the Seminole Wars, the county seat moved frequently, just as it had during territorial times. Finally, at the end of 1856, the settlement of Jernigan (and therefore present-day Orlando) was chosen. In January 1892, after several more moves within Orlando, this redbrick, Victorian-influenced courthouse (shown in 1949) was dedicated. Money for the clock and bells was collected separately from money for the building and tower. Those efforts were led by W. C. Sherman, who had organized the first volunteer fire department in town in 1883. With the $3,000 raised, he hired the manufacturers who made London's Big Ben.

When Orlando was chosen as the seat of Orange County's government, the courthouse was established in an abandoned log cabin that had only a dirt floor and no windows. Court was held there until 1863, when a two-story log structure became available. That building and the records housed there were burned in a fire set on the eve of a cattle-rustling trial in 1868. A frame building replaced that structure, but it was outgrown by 1875. In order to keep the county seat in Orlando, Jacob Summerlin donated $10,000 toward construction of an adequate and "respectable" courthouse. That frame building served until the early 1890s, when it was moved to make way for the 1892 redbrick courthouse, which continued to be used for county office space even after a new courthouse was completed in 1927. In 1959, the red building was condemned and razed, and a modern-style office annex was built on the site. In 1997, a new courthouse and county office tower opened several blocks to the north. After that move, the annex and a connecting tower were demolished for this park of native plants at the entrance to the local history center.

Orange County's 1927 courthouse certainly helped bring downtown Orlando's building stock into the twentieth century. Its architect was Murray S. King, Florida's first registered architect, who had since his arrival in 1904 designed a number of commercial properties and residences, including the Albertson Public Library, the Angebilt Hotel, the Rosalind Club building, the Yowell-Duckworth department store, and the First Presbyterian Church. Unfortunately, the 1927 Orange County Courthouse was his final project; his son James finished supervising the building's progress following his father's death. When the Greek Classical–style building was dedicated on October 12, 1927, it allowed the consolidation of offices from all around Orlando. Cells on the top floor even replaced the county jail. In 1995, the county moved into a twenty-four-story tower, and, shortly after, the 1960 annex and a connecting tower (visible in the background) were demolished.

In the late 1990s, the 1927 courthouse, which originally cost $1 million, underwent a renovation estimated at $30 million before the Historical Society of Central Florida and the History Center moved in. The building houses a restored courtroom, a museum dedicated to showcasing central Florida history, and a collection of central Florida historical resources. This site originally consisted of the L. P. Wescott home. Wescott was a horticulturist who had moved to Orlando from Detroit in 1875. Not surprisingly, he surrounded the large frame house with rare plants and trees from all over the world. He also built a greenhouse on separate property. The garden and greenhouse were regional landmarks, even after Wescott moved to the Rock Lake area and Leslie Pell-Clarke purchased the property. In 1900, Pell-Clarke gave the house to the Episcopal Church, to be used as a home for the bishop. Known as the "Bishopstead," the property was sold to the county in 1924.

The Chamber of Commerce Building at 113 East Central (shown here ca. 1930) was completed in 1927 and served as the chamber's home until 1968, when the organization moved to new quarters near Lake Ivanhoe. Interestingly, the second floor of this building was only a balcony that overlooked the first floor, where trade shows, member exhibits, and programs could be staged; offices were located on the third and fourth floors. Started as the Board of Trade in 1886, the group's focus was to attract visitors and businesses to Orlando. One of its first feats was to revive the city following a yellow fever epidemic in 1888. At news of the outbreak, the board of health forbade any supplies or provisions, mail, or people from entering the county—in effect quarantining the town. Indeed, Orlando was reportedly the only place in the state that did not have an outbreak—not even one case—of yellow fever, but the town had isolated itself and started an economic downturn. To speed recovery, the Board of Trade placed advertisements in major city papers of the time (including Havana, Cuba) to brag about Orlando's situation.

The 1927 chamber headquarters was demolished in 1984 to make room for an expansion of the main public library. The adjacent library building had been erected in 1966 to replace the Charles Albertson Public Library. Albertson had donated his collection of more than 12,000 books (some sources say as many as 15,000) to the citizens of Orlando when plans were announced for a proper library in the early 1920s. The existing building was described by its architect, John M. Johansen, as "a composition in monolithic concrete." Its poured-concrete walls imitated rough-hewn cedar panels. When the expansion opened in 1985, the new walls blended seamlessly with Johansen's textured design. The Orange County Public Library system now serves nearly all of the Orlando area with more than a dozen branches.

This public school building on the south side of Jackson Street, between Orange Avenue and Boone Street, served as Orlando's city hall from 1924 to 1958 (it is shown here in the late 1930s). The site was originally home to the South Florida Institute (sometimes called the Methodist Institute), a grade school that was built in 1883 and operated by the Methodist Episcopal Church. Unfortunately, the institute suffered financial problems and the church struggled to secure funds. The school's name was changed to the Wesleyan Seminary and then the Wesleyan Institute before being abandoned in 1886, when the city acquired the building and property. At that time, it served as a public school for both elementary and high school classes. This larger school building was erected in 1906. It continued to serve the police department until being demolished in 1972 to make a block-square park to honor former mayor William Beardall.

Today, the Lincoln Plaza office tower stands at the southern end of the SunTrust Center Complex (which includes the thirty-story SunTrust Banking Tower, completed in 1988, and the nine-story Park Building). The sixteen-story building brought about the loss of Beardall Park and mandated the closing of Jackson Street, acts that caused a small public outcry. The tower was completed in 2000.

After more than eight years of planning and debating locations, this new $1.6 million city hall was dedicated in October 1958. Need for the new building was partly necessitated by the arrival of the Glenn L. Martin Co. (now known as Martin-Marietta Corp.), which called for road extensions, additional schools, and other services. The Orlando Utilities Commission also moved its expansion plans ahead of schedule in order to guarantee its ability to meet the company's power requirements and water needs. The

1958 city hall building was left in place during the construction of its replacement on the back side of the lot. Its implosion in October 1991 was filmed for use in the movie *Lethal Weapon 3*. The city was excited to let the production company blow up the old city hall—the city was paid $165,000 for the privilege. Following the explosion, then-mayor Bill Frederick played a policeman who said "bravo" to characters Murtaugh and Riggs.

City Hall at City Commons was opened on June 1, 1991. The park area that is the City Commons was completed after the 1958 building was destroyed. The commons has numerous fountains and sculptures, plenty of trees, and many seats and benches for relaxing. Some of the seats are rocking chairs that are located on the building's "front porch," an area to the left of the main entrance. The light tower at the front of this photo is a sixty-foot, illuminated, stainless steel and laminated glass monument created by sculptor Ed Carpenter and installed in 1992. The other buildings surrounding City Commons are office towers—the CNL Center Tower (on the left), completed in 1999, and the newer CNL Center II (on the right). CNL is one of the largest privately held real estate investment and development companies in the United States and is based in the CNL Center Tower.

LAKE EOLA HOTEL ORLANDO FLA. M 325

Near the northeast shore of Lake Eola, this property (shown here ca. 1950) was built in 1922 by Edward Salmon and opened as the Eola Hotel. Soon renamed the Bonnie Villa Hotel, the building was purchased by John S. McEwan and Gaston H. Edwards, who together developed it into the Orlando Clinic. McEwan and Edwards were brothers-in-law and both doctors. McEwan was for many years a leader in the movement to build a modern hospital in Orlando. Toward that goal, he had been a partner in the Harris &

McEwan Hospital and, in 1911, had built and opened his own hospital at Main Street and Central Avenue. When World War I started, McEwan enlisted and left to serve in France, leaving his brother-in-law to manage the hospital. Eventually, Edwards enlisted, too, and left for Italy. He had already served in the Panama Canal Zone and, after the war, served with the American Red Cross in Greece.

By 1932, the building was housing the College of Music, and the YMCA moved to the site in 1954 from its former headquarters on Magnolia Avenue. The structure later served as a retirement home, youth hostel, hotel, and restaurant. A 1999 restoration resulted in seventeen deluxe hotel suites that are managed by a company specializing in unique hospitality concepts in downtown Orlando. The EoInn and Spa has a sister property just a few blocks away on Summerlin Avenue—the Veranda Bed and Breakfast. This entire area was once owned by Jacob Summerlin. Known as both "king of the crackers" and the "cattle king of Florida," Summerlin bought two hundred acres around and including Lake Eola in 1873. In 1883, he offered a strip of land around the lake, including the corner across from this site, to the city, for use as a park. Lake Eola was known at that time as Sandy Beach, or just "the lake." It was Summerlin's son Robert who named the lake after a friend.

The Gifford Arms Hotel Apartments (the two-story building behind the "motor lodge" sign) opened on Colonial Drive west of Lake Dot in November 1937. Several of these "apartment/hotels" were built around this time in easily accessible areas around the central business district to draw seasonal visitors that the locals called "snowbirds"—largely, retirees who came south shortly after Thanksgiving and stayed until nearly Easter. The accompanying motor lodge opened in May 1955 to attract a different kind of visitor that was becoming more prevalent at that time—drivers, taking advantage of road improvements and travel-friendly, reliable automobiles, who drove to the area for only a few days or a week. Several of these motor lodges were built around this time, especially on the major highways that came into town from the north.

The apartment building and motel complex is still in business. Gordon Gifford had moved to Orlando from New York in 1913 and purchased a home overlooking Lake Dot. In 1936, he moved the home around the corner onto Putnam Street, then proceeded to erect the apartment/hotel building on the house's original site. Rooms could be rented individually or as two-room suites. The motel addition offered twenty-four more rooms with adjacent parking. Many similar apartment/hotel properties (like the Cheney Court Apartments, the Allardice Arms Apartment Hotel, Highland Lake Apartments, and the Bayonet Apartments) have been converted into standard apartment units. Most of the early motels (like the Wigwam Village, Flamingo Court, Lake Tyler Motor Inn, the Sands Motel, and Court Cadillac) have gone out of business over the years, though many of the properties have been transformed into easily recognized chain names.

In the early years of mail delivery, the post office often moved as frequently as the postmaster changed. In fact, the post office was usually in the postmaster's home or place of business. In 1871, for example, when Ed W. Speir was postmaster, the post office had been in his building at the corner of Main and Pine; when James Delaney was named postmaster in 1887, it was moved to the Kuhl-Delaney Building on Pine Street. Finally, in 1890, mostly because

the town's businessmen wanted a more central location for it, a neutral space was secured in the San Juan Hotel. In 1917, the first official post office facility was established in a building on the southwest corner of Central Avenue and Court Street. That post office continued to be used until this federal courthouse, office building, and post office (shown shortly after most exterior construction was finished) was dedicated in April 1941.

The 1941 building was renovated in 2003, and the space was divided between the post office and offices for the St. James Catholic Cathedral (which is located next door and once owned the entire block where the cathedral and the post office sit) and the diocese of Orlando. The federal-level courts and most other offices had relocated in the mid-1970s. The 1917 post office was razed in the early 1960s. Since closing as a post office, the building had been used as a warehouse for Ivey's department store, served as the headquarters of the National Youth Administration, and provided recreation space for enlisted men. The federal government had officially established service to the settlement of Jernigan in 1850. That service was changed to Orlando when the new town was recognized in September 1857. The tower in the background of this photograph is the Orange County Courthouse and office tower that opened in 1997.

The Myrtle Shop at the northeast corner of West Church Street and Division Avenue, shown here in the mid- to late-1950s, was one of many businesses in the African American part of Orlando that is now known as the Parramore Heritage Neighborhood. In the late 1800s, African American settlers were working all over Orlando. But they usually went home to one of two areas in town. By the turn of the twentieth century, nearly all of Orlando's black culture had settled into one of those areas: Parramore, which was only six blocks from the main part of town. In the 1930s and 1940s, Parramore had everything it needed to be independent: housing, professional businesses, shops, hotels, churches, and schools—all run by blacks for the black population. Parramore even had its own "downtown" strip. When the Washington Shores development opened farther out of town in the 1940s, the prominent black residents began relocating; many took their amenities with them.

Since the early 1980s, the city of Orlando has tried a number of different methods for dealing with the changing environment in Parramore. Public and private investment projects like this block-long structure that provides new business space and parking, streetscaping efforts, and a renovation program have so far done little except alter the fabric of the district. One of the more positive changes was the opening of the Wells' Built Museum of African American History and Culture in 2000. The museum is set in Orlando's premier black hotel, the Wells' Built Hotel, which opened in 1926. Its builder, William Monroe Wells, was one of the town's first African American doctors. On the far side of Parramore is another successful anchor: the Callahan Community Recreation Center. Callahan was the third home of the Orlando Black School, which grew and split into the largely black Jones High School and the Callahan and Holden elementary schools.

Municipal Auditorium hosted its first performance on February 21, 1927. The building was located at the Livingston Street entrance to the central Florida fair and exposition grounds (which later became Sunshine Park). The area for an official fairgrounds had been established in 1909, and the first official Orange County Fair was held the next February, after a half-mile track and some sheds were installed. That 1910 fair featured the first air flight in the state of Florida, devised to attract attention to the fair—a contest with a prize of $1,500 to any aviator who could stay aloft longer than five minutes. Three contestants entered, but only one succeeded. Lincoln Beachey not only flew longer than the minimum time, he also stayed in town and flew every day of the fair. Beachey was the first man to fly upside down, first in America to master the loop-the-loop, and the first man to tailslide on purpose.

The auditorium is now known as the Robert S. Carr Performing Arts Center, or just the "Bob Carr," and it is one of the structures that makes up the Orlando Centroplex. The Centroplex is a group of public facilities that also includes the Orlando arena (once called the "O-rena," this venue is currently home to the NBA's Magic and the Predators, an arena football team), a small exposition center, Lake Dot Park, and some hotels and restaurants. The Bob Carr's old facade was covered in 1977 by a glass atrium that was built around the front of the building to provide additional lobby space and to increase accessibility. Though the fairgrounds and Sunshine Park are gone, on performance nights, with the interior lights turned on, the original front of the city auditorium glows from inside, as bright as the day it opened.

The first settler in the area north of Orlando that would become Winter Park was David Mizell, who arrived in 1858. By the 1870s, he had been joined by two African American homesteaders, Will Frazier and Charles Williams, and by Wilson Phelps, who had planted 1,400 orange trees, 150 lemon trees, and 300 lime trees. Not until 1881, with the arrival of Loring Chase, did anyone see the potential of this area's natural beauty: its crystal-clear lakes, tall pine forests, fertile wilderness, and favorable winter climate. Chase, a real-estate developer from Chicago who came to the area to treat his chronic bronchitis, saw that potential. In only a few months, land for Florida's first "planned" town had been purchased, surveyed, and platted. By 1888, this was the view looking north up Park Avenue from New England Avenue. The building on the right is the Henkel Building, built by Dr. Miller A. Henkel, "the beloved physician of Winter Park."

The new building on the northeast corner of Park and New England was completed in just the last few years. Across Park Avenue from this block, to the left, is the southern end of Central Park. Central Park consists of a rose garden, a fountain memorial to World War I veterans, a fountain by resident sculptor Albin Polasek, a band shell, the Amtrak train station, several century-old oaks, and blocks and blocks of grass. Chase included land for this park in his original plan for the town, but additional blocks were donated to the city by Charles Hosmer Morse in 1911, one of his many gifts to the people of Winter Park. Morse first bought land on Lake Osceola during his earliest visit, in the winter of 1881–1882. He later bought several citrus groves in the area as well. But he did not take up permanent residence until 1905, when he moved into the former home of Francis Bangs Knowles. He lived there until his death in 1921.

No consideration of the history and growth of Winter Park is complete without considering the influence of the college that sits on the southern end of the town's main street. Instrumental in the history of that school is the First Congregational Church of Winter Park. The Congregational Church first met in the town hall in October 1882, but a congregation was not organized until 1884. The building in this photograph was erected a year later, at the same time the General Congregational Association was deciding to establish an institution of higher learning somewhere in Florida (the Congregationalists established many of the earliest colleges and universities in the United States, including Harvard, Yale, and Dartmouth). In the running were the cities of Jacksonville (then, the state's only "real" city), Daytona Beach, Mount Dora, Orange City, and Winter Park. Winter Park was only a four-year-old village at the time, but its wealthy, winter-only residents from the north managed to compile the most attractive offer.

After the current Congregational Church structure was built in 1924, the bell from the tower of the original building was eventually moved to Knowles Memorial Chapel at Rollins College. Rollins is the oldest institution of higher education in the state, and the state's only school that includes a Nobel Prize winner as a graduate (Donald Cram, class of 1941; Nobel Prize in Chemistry). When Winter Park was chosen as the site for the college, the city's founders gave up a location on Lake Virginia, where a grand resort had been planned. Reverend Edward P. Hooker, the first reverend for the Winter Park group, also served as the first president of the college, which was named after its chief benefactor, Alonzo W. Rollins. Some of the first Rollins classes were held in the Congregational Church, but in six years, the campus had classrooms, men's and women's dormitories, a dining hall, and a gymnasium.

Loring Chase's earliest maps and sales brochures depicted a gridded network of planned streets and boulevards lined with trees and new homes. The backbone of the town was to be Park Avenue (above right), which provided frontage for the business district. The Boulevard (above left), now Morse Boulevard, was to provide a direct route from the Seminole Hotel resort property on Lake Osceola to the South Florida Railroad train depot. Interlachen Avenue connected Lake Maitland with Lake Virginia.

Another route followed the lakeshore east to Osceola (known as Lake View before 1870) and the Mizell homestead. This route also wandered to the west and south, as Orange Avenue, to Orlando. The Shepherd Hardware Building (above), now the Parkwood Building, was built in 1912 on the southeast corner of the Boulevard and Park Avenue. It was only the second brick commercial building in town.

Still in use, the Parkwood Building has changed little over the years. Neither, so you would think, have the streets! Winter Park first began paving its streets with brick in 1915 as automobiles became more common. Eventually, those streets were replaced or paved over with asphalt and concrete to provide smoother rides. Between 1998 and 2000, however, many hard-surfaced streets in central Winter Park were repaved with brick (in some cases, the asphalt or concrete was simply removed to uncover the still-underlying bricks) to aid in rainwater recovery efforts—the uneven, unmortared brick-and-sand surface helps to slow, absorb, and filter some of the dirty, oily water that floods the roadways during heavy Florida rains. With hard surfaces such as asphalt or concrete, rainwater is dumped directly into storm sewers that drain into area lakes.

The Hamilton Hotel (the entire left side of this 1924 photograph) opened on Park Avenue in 1922 on the site of the old Winter Park Hotel, a three-story frame building. A small lobby near the far end of the building led to fifty sleeping rooms upstairs, some with balconies overlooking Park Avenue, while numerous shops occupied space on the first floor. Located only a block from the city train depot, the Hamilton Hotel usually housed passengers during layovers and businessmen who were passing through town—not the members of the wealthy northern elite who stayed at other hotels in Winter Park while looking into setting up winter residences in town. The Hamilton Hotel was also one of the early homes to Rollins Press, a publishing house established in 1917 to produce copies of papers and creative works written by Rollins students.

The Hamilton Hotel building was renovated and renamed the Park Plaza Hotel in 1977. It now hosts several restaurants, sidewalk cafés, and shops. Park Avenue, sometimes called simply "the avenue," has always been the primary street for business and shopping in the area of the original Winter Park—that went according to the original plan for the town. Nearly all of the structures along the street were built in the 1910s, 1920s, and 1930s. Newer buildings have been made to fit into the appearance and atmosphere of the district (except, some would say, for the current city hall and the Amtrak station). Clothing, housewares, cooking goods, all varieties of food and beverage—the avenue is a district all its own. All that is missing is the cinema, which once stood next to the Hamilton Hotel. The Colony Theater opened in 1940 but lost business to the suburbs by the 1970s, when it was home to the first Barnie's Coffee and Tea Company shop.

Knowles Memorial Chapel was completed in 1932, after only a year of construction. At that time it was located in the center of the campus. The chapel was a gift to the college made in memory of Francis Bangs Knowles, one of the founders and original trustees of Rollins College. It was designed by Ralph Adams Cram, who also designed the Church of St. John the Divine in New York City and the chapel on the campus of the University of Notre Dame. The gift also included installation of a custom pipe organ. The Skinner organ was expanded in 1955 and completely renovated between 1998 and 2001. In 1999, a freestanding antiphonal organ was installed in the rear of the balcony surrounding the Rose Window. The building continues the Spanish-Mediterranean Renaissance design that is featured throughout the Rollins campus.

The chapel building was placed on the National Register of Historic Places in 1997. Six months later, the adjacent and adjoining Annie Russell Theatre was placed on the register. Also designed by Cram, the theater is named after stage actress Annie Russell, who retired from Broadway to form her own stage company, which enabled her to improvise new techniques. She was among the first, for example, to use electric bulbs for stage lighting and to experiment with colored lighting. Her productions toured the United States, Britain, and the Caribbean. After her second retirement, she ended up in Winter Park and took an interest in the productions at Rollins. At the time, many of them were performed at a small stage in town. Soon after Russell's arrival, Louise Curtis Bok offered to build the college a proper facility if her friend was allowed to be active in the program.

The city of Sanford, founded in 1870, sits on the southern shore of Lake Monroe. Only a few years before this photograph was taken, Sanford had been just a small outpost known as the "southern edge of civilization," the southernmost point for steamboat travel up the St. John's River from Jacksonville, which was the gateway to the rest of the East Coast via the Atlantic Ocean. As more homesteaders arrived to settle interior lands, Sanford gained importance as a steamer port—with more inland areas developing, the need for importing supplies and exporting products became even more urgent. By the mid-1880s, about the date of this photo, rail service had become a second, but no less important, method of transporting goods and people. Surprisingly, the two modes of transportation existed, complementary and competitive, side by side, until the trucking industry started taking an edge on both in the late 1920s.

In September 1887, a bakery caught fire, and before the volunteer fire department could bring the blaze under control, most of the wooden structures in that part of town were burned. When the area was rebuilt, the new structures were made of masonry, like the one seen here on the right. After its prominent past as the gateway to what was once considered southern Florida and its quick growth around the turn of the 1900s, the core city of Sanford went largely unchanged for much of the twentieth century. Its large residences, intact commercial buildings, and streets shaded by live oaks full of Spanish moss were rediscovered late in the century when Sanford served as a setting for parts of several movies, including the infamous coming-of-age film *My Girl* in 1991, *Passenger 57* in 1992, *Rosewood* in 1997, and Academy Award and Golden Globe winner *Monster* in 2003. Today, Sanford has two historic districts listed on the National Register of Historic Places: a commercial district consisting of twenty-six buildings and a residential district with 434 houses.

In 1870, Henry Shelton Sanford purchased land west of Mellonville. He organized a land company, built a 600-foot-long pier into the lake, established telegraph service, and erected a two-hundred-room hotel. The bustling new town incorporated in 1877 and absorbed Mellonville six years later. With the beginning of rail service in 1880, Sanford solidified its position as a regional transportation center. Before long, the South Florida Railroad had built a wharf into the lake to unload steamers directly as well as a rail yard that included a locomotive roundtable, a car manufacturing facility, and a steam engine repair shop. In spite of the tranquility shown in this photograph, circa 1886, the wharves in Sanford provided employment for hundreds of men working to transfer goods from boat to train or vice versa, to warehouse goods, to process meat and fish, and to operate stores and stables. Women worked nearby in restaurants and lunchrooms, and as maids in boardinghouses. By the turn of the 1900s, in addition to arriving and departing steamboats, twenty-five trains ran through the town daily.

By the coming of the next century, trucking had erased virtually all signs of Sanford's early glory as the port and transportation hub to central Florida. Most of the rails have been taken up inside the city, and the wharves that remain stand neglected and detached from the shore. The warehouses and transfer houses, liveries and stables, and markets and rooming houses are all gone, too. In 2003, a multimillion-dollar renovation and redevelopment project began along the city's lakefront. That same year, a new bridge opened across the St. John's River and western Lake Monroe. It carries an ever-increasing number of automobiles and trucks past Sanford along the interstate highway.

The town of Eatonville was incorporated in August 1887 by former slaves and African American workers. It is today recognized as the oldest incorporated all-black town in the United States. Most of the founders of the community that was to become Eatonville arrived in Maitland after the Civil War to clear land for crops and citrus groves; work in turpentine mills; help build houses, business structures, and hotels; and lay track for new railways. In 1881, these residents of Maitland decided they wanted their own place of worship, a gathering place separate from the white congregation. The group initially called their congregation the African Methodist Church, but they soon decided to honor the man who donated the land for a building by renaming themselves the Lawrence Church of Maitland. They later became the St. Lawrence African Methodist Episcopal Church, the name that remains today. A small building (which later served as a library and then a residence) was built in 1882. As the town and the congregation grew, this larger building was erected in 1909.

After outgrowing the 1909 sanctuary, the congregation planned for a third structure. The last service was held in the old building in September 1968; the first service in the new structure was held in August 1972. As with the second building, the interior of the new sanctuary is graced with a series of unique paintings, presented by the Maitland Art Center, that depict Psalms 23. The paintings are unique because the Biblical characters are represented by persons of African descent. In 1987, Eatonville—which was named for Maitland Mayor Josiah Eaton, who was instrumental in the land deal that provided 112 acres for the town—celebrated its centennial with eight months of activities. Included were parades and festivals, hosting the annual National Conference of Black Mayors, and a tribute to Zora Neale Hurston, a precursor to January's annual Zora! Festival. Hurston was an author and resident of Eatonville who was one of the brightest lights of the Harlem Renaissance of the 1930s.

The Dillard-Boyd Block, which housed the Winter Garden Pharmacy during the Christmas season in 1915, sits at the oddly shaped intersection of Plant and Main streets in Winter Garden. Winter Garden was one of the communities that sprang up around Lake Apopka. The settlement's location was distinct for three reasons. First, the lake was large enough to influence the weather: it cooled the air in the summer and warmed it in the winter. Second, the land along the south shore was unusually high, dry, and also fertile. Third, the surrounding woods were filled with game, in particular wild hogs and free-range poultry and cattle. The first settlers in the area began farming their homestead grants in 1857. They were subsistence farmers who grew their own corn, sweet potatoes, and other vegetables and raised sugarcane and cotton for cash. Corn was also sold to ranchers in the southern part of the state.

Winter Garden's growth was greatly impacted by the arrival of the Orange Belt Railway in the late 1880s. When that line was completed, the town was linked to the rail and shipping center of Sanford to the east and Tampa and St. Petersburg to the west. Trains brought sport fishermen and trophy hunters from all over the country to fish camps and marinas on the state's second-largest lake. Bass and other fish, wild game, wilderness excursions, citrus and other exotic tropical plants, winter warmth—these were the attractions that drew Northerners until about 1930. Then, suddenly, Lake Apopka lost its luster: raw sewage from development around the lake, untreated waste from surrounding citrus processors, and damming and draining for farmland were the underlying problems that led to the end of area tourism. The area's economy now relies on a variety of industrial ventures and its proximity to Orlando and Disney World.

Apopka, to the northwest of Orlando proper, had erected Apopka Union School in 1901. That six-room building, along with much of the town, was destroyed in what became known as the Cyclone of 1918. As soon as money could be raised, this elementary school and a neighboring high school were built. The word *Apopka* is an English interpretation of the Native American word for the area that sounded more like "Ahapapka." White settlers entered the area after the Second Seminole War (1835–1842) and passage of the

Armed Occupation Act of 1842 that granted 160 acres to anyone who would agree to stay on the land and "protect" it from the natives. Life in the 1850s and 1860s centered around the Masons and their lodge, which was completed in 1859—the settlement even became known as the Lodge. The town was incorporated in 1882 as Apopka City, which was shortened to Apopka five years later.

Apopka's newest city hall stands on the site of the old Apopka High School. Earlier city halls opened in 1915 (built of masonry, that building was one of the few structures left after the Cyclone of 1918) and 1935 (that building was erected with WPA labor and provided space for offices, a community auditorium, and the police department). Apopka is now the second-largest city in Orange County after Orlando and owes its latest growth to easy access to and from Disney World. Earlier growth was spurred by proximity to Lake Apopka and advertising campaigns that capitalized on the lake's reputation as a fisherman's paradise to draw sport fishermen from the North. The city also owes past spurts to the fern and foliage industries—by 1924, the city had adopted the "Fern City" as its nickname; after the Great Depression, ferneries diversified into indoor plants. The outlying area is still marketed as the foliage-growing capital of the world.

One of the Orlando area's National Register sites, this building was dedicated to house Longwood's Christ Episcopal Church congregation on Easter Sunday 1882. It is the oldest existing church structure in Seminole County and is still in use. Land was donated by Edward Warren Henck, who settled the area and named the town. Henck had traveled to Mellonville (present-day Sanford) by steamer in 1871, but after spending two nights in that town's "so-called hotel," he headed south on foot. Fifteen miles later, he found a site on Myrtle Lake that he began homesteading. Henck helped locate a plausible rail route that included Longwood, Maitland, Winter Park, and Orlando on the line that was being built to link the steamer port at Sanford with developing towns to the south. Rail traffic soon brought waves of wealthy Northerners— vacationers, winter residents, and investors—to Longwood as promotional materials bragged that the area was free of malaria and had all that was needed to provide "perfect health." In only a few years, the town had a population of more than 1,000 and boasted three hotels.

The historic church's square bell tower, vertical board-and-batten paneled siding, and simple exterior design were typical of the first churches in central Florida. The Longwood structure was renovated in 1965, then moved about a hundred feet to the east in 1988. When built, most of the construction costs, including revenue for the stained-glass windows (on the front of the chapel), were raised by the Boston family of Frederic H. Rand, a Civil War veteran who arrived in Longwood in 1876 and planted a citrus grove. At the time, citrus was one of the three leading industries in the area, along with turpentine and lumber. Rand later moved north to the developing town of Sanford, where he became the general passenger agent for E. W. Henck's South Florida Railroad, which had extended west from Kissimmee to Lakeland and Tampa.

South of Orlando is the city of Kissimmee, the county seat of Osceola County. The Brandow Brothers' Opera House, shown here in 1887, provided space for community gatherings, the post office, and government offices. It is said to have attracted nationally known performers and to have drawn audiences from as far away as Narcoosee, but it was destroyed by fire in 1920. Kissimmee was originally known as Allendale, and the main street served as a cow path over which cattle were driven from grazing lands that ranged all across the western part of the state on their way to Sanford for shipping. Kissimmee sits along the shore of Lake Tohopekaliga. *Tohopekaliga* is an English translation of a Native American word for "protected place," so known because the Seminole Indians used the islands of the lake as homes for their women and children; the waters of the lake served as a buffer that protected them from white, Indian-hunting soldiers.

Makinson's hardware store is the second-oldest business enterprise in Kissimmee and now occupies at least part of the Opera House site. The Opera House sat on Broadway, which was famous at one time for its broad-boarded walkways and for being paved in Bermuda grass! According to local historians, the road was turfed all the way across and was kept neat and cropped by free-roaming, family-owned cows that grazed there by day and slept there at night. The three-story Tropical Hotel, which stood nearby on Broadway, was said to provide the finest quarters south of Jacksonville. The growing town needed such a place after Hamilton Disston's river dredging and land reclamation efforts proved successful, because wealthy merchants, hunters, and environmentalists frequently stopped at the new port before heading south to Lake Okeechobee, the Everglades, and the Gulf of Mexico.

When Disney representatives began to purchase tracts of vacant, undeveloped land in Orange and Osceola counties in 1964, they made no announcements. Instead, the small purchases that gradually accumulated to more than 27,000 acres were kept secret for more than a year. The Disney Company now held more than forty square miles in central Florida, more than twice the land area of Manhattan. This aerial photo shows Bay Lake in June 1967, which would become the centerpiece of the first theme park. The inset photo shows Roy Disney and the "Project X" development team surveying the area prior to the 1965 announcement. Speculation had grown as to who was acquiring the massive land parcel, and the Orlando Sentinel guessed right in October 1965. Walt, Roy, and Governor W. Haydon Burns held a press conference to announce the project on November 15, 1965, at the Cherry Plaza Hotel in Orlando. Once the news was out, land prices jumped from $183 an acre to $1,000 an acre overnight.

Once the announcement was made, the vast civil engineering project began. General Joe Potter, formerly of the Army Engineering Corps, spearheaded the transformation of swamp and wetland into the world's largest theme park. Forty-seven miles of meandering drainage canals were built along with twenty-two miles of levees and a series of pumping stations. Bay Lake was cleared of weeds, while an adjacent 186-acre wetland site was dredged to form the Seven Seas Lagoon (above) linked to Bay Lake. Soil from the dredging enabled engineers to raise the height of the land across the Magic Kingdom site by fourteen feet and create a network of "utilidor" (utility/corridor) tunnels for staff access. Bay Lake was completely drained of its 3.5 billion gallons of water, and a layer of sediment eight feet thick was removed. Underneath the centuries-old grime, they found sand, which was excavated and used around the shoreline. Today, Disney's Florida theme parks have generated a statewide industry and made Florida the theme-park capital of the world.

Cinderella Castle at the Magic Kingdom, shown here shortly after completion in July 1971, is nearly twice the size of the Sleeping Beauty Castle at Disneyland in Anaheim, California. Like its counterpart, the castle's designers applied an artistic technique called "forced perspective" to the beauty of real European castles to make higher points, such as the spires, appear farther away than they actually are. There are twenty-seven different towers, which are numbered from one to twenty-nine—towers thirteen and seventeen were not constructed when it was realized they couldn't be seen by anyone in the park. The castle was built as a visual magnet, high enough to be seen from the point where guests alight from the ferry at the Seven Seas Lagoon and splendid enough to draw people down Main Street USA.

Though it changed very little in its first twenty-five years, in recent times the castle has become a hotspot for celebrating Disney's special events. In 1996 it was transformed into a glaring eighteen-story birthday cake to celebrate the twenty-fifth anniversary of the Walt Disney World Resort. The giant candy canes and sugar-coating effects lasted a whole fifteen months. For the "Happiest Celebration on Earth" to celebrate Disneyland's fiftieth birthday, it was royally decked out with swags, banners, and tapestries, the exterior adorned with golden statues of Peter Pan characters along with many other Disney animation favorites. The most visible change was a huge mirror modeled on the magic mirror used by the witch in *Snow White and the Seven Dwarfs* erected above the front archway, which was not removed until September 2006.

The Orlando site, on the borders of Orange and Osceola counties, was one of three Florida locations under consideration by Roy Disney's Project X team (pictured above). The huge area of land that the Disney brothers eventually bought gave their company a massive, future-proof estate. Walt had always lamented the fact that Disneyland in Anaheim was surrounded by low-rent motels that had hiked their prices to take advantage of Disney visitors. The land acquisition would give them the space to develop a range of accommodations for visitors that would enhance the experience of a trip to Disney World. The three key land acquisitions were 12,400 acres owned by a group of Orlando home builders, 1,250 acres owned by a local investment group, and 8,500 acres owned by state senator Irlo Bronson. The jigsaw pattern of land purchases was traced onto a map at Disney headquarters in Los Angeles, which Walt was said to check daily. Only when all the pieces were in place was the announcement made.

Though Walt's true interest in developing in Florida was his EPCOT venture—right up until the time of his death, he was immersing himself in books on urban planning—Florida state's cooperation had been essential, and they wanted the Magic Kingdom first. The 1971 theme park was followed by EPCOT Center in 1982, Disney/MGM Studios in 1989, and the fourth major theme park, Animal Kingdom (above), in 1998. At over 500 acres, Animal Kingdom is Disney's biggest theme park. Disney's ambition of providing high-quality accommodations to its guests has been fully realized with a succession of themed resorts on the land that Roy surveyed back in 1964. Guests can now choose from Old Key West Resort, Port Orleans Resort, Dixie Landings Resort, Typhoon Lagoon Resort, Caribbean Beach Resort, Fort Wilderness Resort, and the Walt Disney All-Star Resort. Though Walt never got to build his experimental community, his forward thinking has helped the Disney corporation realize at least part of his vision.

Walt Disney's original intention for EPCOT was to be his Experimental Prototype Community of Tomorrow. His new town would "take its cue from the new ideas and new technologies that are now emerging from the creative centers of American industry." His death in 1966 left the Disney Corporation with a lot of Florida land and no driving force to establish his vision. And so instead of an experimental community, the EPCOT Center was built as a showcase for science and technology, combined with internationally themed areas, known respectively as Future World and World Showcase. The iconic building of EPCOT was the eighteen-story geodesic dome, Spaceship Earth, similar to the dome Buckminster Fuller had designed as the American Pavilion for Expo 67 in Montreal. Official groundbreaking on the site began on October 1, 1979, and Disney's second Florida theme park opened its doors to visitors precisely three years later.

EPCOT Center went through a series of name changes until it was eventually shortened to plain Epcot in 1996. To celebrate the millennium, the dome gained a twenty-five-story wand modeled on the wand used by Mickey Mouse in the animated feature *Fantasia*. Though intended only to last a year, it remains there still, the figure 2000 replaced by an Epcot sign. The German electronics firm Siemens took on the sponsorship of the Spaceship Earth ride in 2005 after its AT&T sponsorship ended in 2003. Sponsorship is a feature of many of the exhibits in the theme park. In the World Showcase, the "countries" of Italy, France, Germany, Norway, Morocco, the UK, China, Japan, and Canada are sponsored by their national tourist boards. Russia, Spain, and Israel declined to sponsor their pavilions and so never made it past the planning stage; Norway and Morocco were only added later.